UNLOCKING THE POTENTIAL OF PUZZLE-BASED LEARNING

UNLOCKING THE POTENTIAL OF PUZZLE-BASED LEARNING

DESIGNING ESCAPE ROOMS + GAMES FOR THE CLASSROOM

SCOTT NICHOLSON
LIZ CABLE

SAGE Publications Ltd
1 Oliver's Yard
55 City Road
London EC1Y 1SP

CORWIN
A SAGE company
2455 Teller Road
Thousand Oaks, California 91320
(0800)233-9936
www.corwin.com

SAGE Publications India Pvt Ltd
B 1/I 1 Mohan Cooperative Industrial Area
Mathura Road
New Delhi 110 044

SAGE Publications Asia-Pacific Pte Ltd
3 Church Street
#10-04 Samsung Hub
Singapore 049483

Editor: James Clark
Assistant editor: Diana Alves
Production editor: Tanya Szwarnowska
Copyeditor: Salia Nessa
Proofreader: Neil Dowden
Marketing manager: Dilhara Attygalle
Cover design: Wendy Scott
Typeset by: Cenveo Publisher Services
Printed in the UK

First published 2021

Library of Congress Control Number: 2020939016

British Library Cataloguing in Publication data

A catalogue record for this book is available from the British Library

ISBN 978-1-5297-1409-8
ISBN 978-1-5297-1408-1 (pbk)

CONTENTS

About the Authors vii
Acknowledgments ix
Online Resources xi

Introduction 1

1 A framework for learning with escape games 7

2 Game shapes 25

3 World design 45

4 Creating and sharing the narrative 53

5 Concepts for puzzle design 63

6 Designing specific puzzle types 85

7 Designing the escape game experience 105

8 Prototyping and playtesting 119

9 Running the game: facilitation, reflection, and assessment 129

10 Sample game: 'Misinformation Literacy' 141

Components 155

Index 179

ABOUT THE AUTHORS

Dr. Scott Nicholson is a Professor in the Game Design and Development program at Wilfrid Laurier University in Brantford, Ontario, Canada. He has been designing live-action games for over 30 years and was the first scholar to explore escape rooms at an international level. He led a team of students to create the escape rooms for the 2017 and 2019 Red Bull Mind Gamers Escape Room World Championships, and was the designer of the award-winning Breakout EDU puzzle box game *Ballot Box Bumble*. He is a former librarian and library school professor, and his passion is creating face-to-face games for learning in museums, libraries, classrooms, and the home.

Liz Cable is a Senior Lecturer in Digital Narratives and Transmedia Production at Leeds Trinity University, UK, and a PhD candidate researching escape games in education. She founded The Adventurers Guild national live-action role-playing society, was editor of *The Adventurer* magazine, and has run several massive multiplayer campaigns over 30 years. She has been designing commercial and educational escape games since 2015, and teaches educators to make immersive games for the classroom and beyond.

ACKNOWLEDGMENTS

We would like to thank our playtesting families:

Mei, Aileen and Lee-Fay Low,
Leon, Reuben and Toby Jones, and
Zachary and Pauline Shostack

for playtesting the sample game.

ONLINE RESOURCES

The final chapter of this book contains everything you need to run a sample escape game called 'Misinformation Literacy.' While you can photocopy the content from the book and run the game, we also have put the content online so that you can print it out and copy it more easily. You will still need the facilitation guide in the book to run the game, as the game setup and answers will not be found in these printable resources.

In addition, you will find a basic version of the game that can be played via a web browser. There are images for the challenges and validated entry forms for the players to supply the answers. It is not as immersive as the paper-based game; it is more difficult for players to work together on the tasks when gathered around a screen. In addition, you will still need to facilitate the game and the reflection, as the online version is designed to be used in conjunction with the facilitation guide in the book. The online version is not designed as a stand-alone game to be used instead of running a facilitated game experience.

These resources can be found at http://scottnicholson.com/misinformation

INTRODUCTION

As the students filter in, their eyes light up with surprise. Their desks have been moved into clusters and at the center of each cluster is a large box with multiple locks and a sealed envelope. Orchestral music reminiscent of an adventure movie fills the room. As the students take their seats, excitement is in the air. The teacher, with a twinkle in their eye, lowers the music and says:

> 'Welcome, and thank you for coming. We need your help. We have recovered these boxes from Benjamin Franklin's office and have only 30 minutes to get them open before a meeting with our funders. We need your help to explore Franklin's notes and see if you can find the codes needed to get the box open. If you need help, raise your hand and I'll see what I can do. Good luck, and begin!'
>
> A 30-minute countdown clock appears on the screen and begins to tick. The students tear open the envelopes to find a set of plans for some of Franklin's inventions. Over the next half an hour, the students learn about some of the things that Franklin designed, build small models, decrypt hidden messages, and open the locks, one by one, until they open the box to discover what is inside – an open question about the ethics of the use of one of Franklin's inventions. Each group has a different case, which then leads to a discussion of inventions over the years that were not used for their original purpose.

What you have just read is an example of an escape game, where teams of students work together through a series of challenges based on learning objectives designed to explore a real-world topic under a tight time limit. The commercial escape room industry has seen explosive growth over the last few years, and they are appearing in museums and libraries. Escape games take the concepts from escape rooms and repackage them into a format easier for teachers to implement as a classroom activity. Bringing escape games to the classroom allows students to experience these games while learning real-world concepts and developing communication and teamwork skills, and enjoying a different way of exploring course content.

WHAT ARE ESCAPE ROOMS?

> Escape rooms are live action team-based games where players discover clues, solve puzzles, and accomplish tasks in one or more rooms in order to accomplish a specific goal (usually escaping from the room) in a limited amount of time. (Nicholson, 2016: 1)

To start, we will unpack this definition and talk about the key elements of escape rooms. While most games have players control an avatar on the screen or move a piece on a game board, in a live action game, the players and the avatars are one and the same. Escape rooms are one type of live action game where the players play themselves in the game space. Live action role-playing games, otherwise known as LARPs, are live action games where the players are taking on a role of a character in the narrative. Murder mystery games are live action events where the expectation of players to take on a role are lighter than in a LARP. While players are still playing a role, typically of a detective trying to figure out whodunnit, the players are usually playing themselves in the role of a detective. These games are more about the players figuring out who committed the crime than about the players engaging with each other as characters with backstories. In this way, escape rooms are similar to murder mystery games.

One of the reasons that escape rooms are popular is that they are cooperative games where the players work as a team to win the game. Team-based games are powerful in education because they encourage the players to vocalize their thinking and share their explorations of the topic. Social constructionism, first explored by Berger and Luckman (1966), is the theory that the way we think about the world comes out of our co-exploration of the world with others and supports why team-based games are useful models for educational games. In order to succeed as a team, the players should communicate, cooperate, divide-up tasks, and delegate.

Searching the room is the first activity in an escape room. Rather than all the puzzles being out in the open, the players start with a discovery phase where they explore the room, find what is hidden, what is locked, and make preliminary connections between room elements. A core design concept in escape rooms is to take a puzzle, separate the puzzle into different clues and components, and then hide those throughout the room. It might be as simple as finding the clues in a diary and realizing they apply to the protrusions on the walls, or a much more complex solution involving cross-referencing books, decoding messages, finding tools, and then following the decoded directions to use the tools to progress.

This sense of discovery is one of the more powerful emotional aspects of escape rooms. At the start of the game, the players know very little about the space they are in. As they explore the space, they better understand how it is configured and what secrets it hides. At this point, they shift to working through the challenges until they hit a point where they can't progress and then they return to searching the space. In some ways, the escape room is like a treasure hunt, where the players alternate between solving challenges and then following directions to then find the next challenge.

While puzzles are activities that focus on the mental, there can also be activities that focus on the physical. For this book, we use the term 'challenge' to refer to any activity in an escape game. Physical activities can also have mental elements, but a key difference is that in a physical activity, there is an activity that needs to be accomplished even after the players figure out what to do. For example, in a chemistry game, the players could have access to a safety enclosure that is only accessible through rubber gloves attached to the sides. The players may figure out which three chemicals need to be mixed, but if the chemicals are all in different parts of the safety enclosure, the team then needs to work together from different sides of the enclosure to transfer the chemicals to a central location. In escape rooms, most players end up remembering physical activities that they were engaged in, and the shared moments they produce, more than they remember solving an engaging puzzle. One reason is that the process of accomplishing a physical activity is broad and visual, so that members of the team not directly accomplishing that challenge can still watch the process in a way that they can't watch someone solve a mental puzzle.

Another form of challenge in escape games are role-playing challenges. In a role-playing challenge, the players are asked to take on a role different from who they are and engage with the game through verbal and physical interactions. Role-playing challenges usually involve an interaction between a player and someone who is playing a character from the game world, known as a non-player character (NPC), although a role-playing challenge can also come between two or more players, each of whom has a different role in the game. In the most common type of role-playing challenge, the character has a key piece of information that the player needs to continue the game and it is up to the player to ask the right questions, provide a desired payment, prove their worth, or otherwise convince the character to convey the information. More complex role-playing challenges may require players with different roles, goals, and resources to come to a compromise where everyone gets some of what they are seeking, and sacrifice other things. As many players do not seek out role-playing challenges, they should be used sparingly when they are the best tool to bring about a learning outcome, such as gaining empathy, understanding the social side of a complex situation, or simulating how to engage with other people appropriately in a time of crisis.

One type of challenge that is rarely found in recreational escape rooms, but may be appropriate for an educational escape game, is a research challenge. In recreational escape rooms, one of the rules of the design is that the players have access to everything they need to overcome the challenge in the game and that very little outside knowledge is needed. For educational escape games, however, the learning outcome may dictate that the players need to learn how to do research to better understand or resolve a challenge. As escape games can be simulations of real-world challenges that do not come with instructions, requiring the players to do research as part of the game will better prepare them for being successful when they need to use what they have learned.

It is important to note that these challenges do not need to be discrete. A challenge for a physics lesson on how sounds are created could start with a role-playing challenge, where the players get the access code to a safe from a NPC in exchange for a promise of a portion of the reward inside. The players find that the keypad buttons on the safe no longer function. They talk to the NPC again and learn that the keypad made sounds and it was the sounds that triggered the safe. They do research and learn that the keypad buttons generate a tone and then need to do research to learn how to build a tone generator out of the electrical parts around the room. They have to convert the code into the sounds using a tone generator and then play the tones to the safe to overcome the challenge, which opens the next part of the game.

Rather than expose players to all of the challenges at once, escape rooms use doors and locks to divide up the challenges into smaller subsets of challenges in different rooms. Escape games in classrooms can use similar design concepts through containers. Players may be presented with one or more envelopes to start (some of which might contain additional envelopes) as well as a locked box. Upon unlocking the box, the players may be surprised to find another set of envelopes and another locked box. They might also be sent to another physical space where their challenges continue. As the players move through the challenges, they could find an encoding method or a tool like a magnifying glass and the encouragement to return to earlier content to explore it in a different way.

These are all examples of a key concept for this book – creating gates. *Gates* are barriers in the game preventing players from seeing content until the gate is opened by succeeding at one or more challenges. The primary advantage to gating content is that it prevents players from being overwhelmed. If the players are faced with too many things at once, they can easily get confused as to what components and which locks go with which challenges. That said, if the challenges are presented in a purely linear fashion and are not designed to engage the entire team, then some of the team members may have to look on while other team members work on the challenge. Having gated content allows the designer to indicate to the players which challenges should be worked on first, can allow for the development of narrative, and allow for more challenging learning outcomes that depend upon learning outcomes explored earlier in the game. Gating the content so that challenges are grouped allows for the development of a three-act structure, can allow for 'end of level' summation and formative feedback, or allow for a natural pause to take place with the story resuming at a later date. These concepts are explored in-depth in future chapters in this book.

Escape rooms are games driven by their time limits. At the heart of the game is the ticking clock, which for many players is the main tool for generating tension in the room. A ticking clock causes a problem with challenges designed to bring about a learning outcome. Players facing a time limit will take a shortcut to get to the answer of a puzzle without following all of the steps. One way to alleviate this problem is through putting aside some of the class time for the game for reflection, where players are no longer working on the game in a tight time limit, but are able to reflect and discuss what they explored. This will allow students who skipped puzzles or did not complete challenges to learn from those who did, so can ensure that all students have at least some exposure to the learning outcomes.

EDUCATIONAL ESCAPE GAMES VS. COMMERCIAL ESCAPE ROOMS

Ten ways that an educational escape game may differ from a traditional commercial escape room:

1. The nature of the story may not be to escape, but to understand and solve a problem.
2. Challenges can rely on the students bringing prior knowledge into the escape game.
3. Items in the game may be used more than once, as players collect artifacts that help them solve the bigger story and use them in a real-world setting. Most commercial rooms follow a design aesthetic that each item is used only once.
4. Games can be run for much bigger teams or several teams at once using a variety of game shapes.
5. The facilitator may take on a role, or more than one role in the story world.
6. Locks might be memetic with the facilitator gating access to the next challenges based on whether the correct code has been reported.
7. The escape game is situated in an ongoing curriculum with wraparound activities to ensure the most is made of the learning opportunities provided. In this way, the time and effort of designing and setting up the game has the most payback for learner and teacher.
8. The game can include use of proprietary systems and learning portals at an institution.
9. The game can have alternative endings depending on success or failure, or on narrative choices made by the team, but all endings need to reach the same learning outcomes.
10. Creative and open responses can be the outcome of the game, rather than the closed ending of a door that either unlocks or doesn't.

CONCLUSION

Dedicated spaces for escape room games, by their nature, don't fit very well with a classroom setting. Class sizes are too large, classrooms are too small and underfunded, and timetables are too inflexible to allow for small teams to play an escape room without disruption. The route we are exploring is to use different models based on an escape room, called 'escape games', for delivering the content. During the rest of this book, we will pull examples and use design concepts from different types of escape games and present different forms for these games that we call 'game shapes'. Trying to use a traditional escape room structure in a classroom is likely to fail in several ways, which can leave students frustrated and a teacher that doesn't want to try this again. Therefore, it is our hope that by tapping a wide variety of puzzle-based and escape-game design models, we will help you to be more successful in being able to select the game shapes that will help you be effective in bringing about learning outcomes.

REFERENCES

Berger, P. and Luckmann, T. (1966). *The Social Construction of Reality: A Treatise in the Sociology of Knowledge*. New York: Anchor Books.

Nicholson, S. (2016) The state of escape: escape room design and facilities. Paper presented at Meaningful Play 2016. Lansing, MI.

1 A FRAMEWORK FOR LEARNING WITH ESCAPE GAMES

Early adopters of escape games in the classroom quickly discovered how much energy they generate in class but often used them in a one-dimensional way for group building and introductions on a social level, or inductions into an educational setting. Some tested knowledge through puzzles that were little more than re-worked worksheets with padlocks to check answers. Others were used to introduce reflection and peer assessment, with all the learning happening after the game ended. However, it is possible to cover several modes of learning in an escape game and tie the different narrative elements such as the story and the setting into relevant learning objectives.

The framework in Table 1.1 enables the setting of specific learning objectives and individual learning outcomes for students in an escape game; mapping them against both puzzle types and narrative purpose in order to build a cohesive interactive story that provides learning opportunities. To address more than one learning objective, an individual challenge within the game can be designed to fit into one or more of these non-exclusive aspects or sit in a natural overlap of two or more.

Knowledge as a learning outcome is not part of this framework as these concepts run through all of the puzzles and challenges. It is accepted practice that any knowledge needed to solve the puzzles in a commercial escape room will be provided within that room, for example the periodic table, the music scale, a plan of the campus. However, you may be wanting to test or assess the student on what they know

Table 1.1 A framework for learning with escape games

Dimension	Scope	Role of the Facilitator / In-Game Ally
Setting	Induction Situated learning Physical layout Real-world location	Real-world roles or playing themselves e.g. librarians in a library answering queries
Social	Teamwork Collaboration and cooperation Communication skills	Collaborators e.g. lab assistant of the missing professor.
Story	Inquiry-based learning Role playing and negotiation Critical thinking	Antagonists and protagonists e.g. the inventor and a rival inventor
Skills	Practice Application Levels of difficulty	Models, patients, and customers e.g. patient needing bloods to be taken
Strategy	Problem-based learning Analysis and synthesis Cognitive strategies Handling complexity	Mentors, sounding boards, and critical friends e.g. artificial intelligence (AI) personal assistant
Simulation	Physical constraints Realistic time constraints Tools and processes	Stakeholders, rule enforcers, and quest givers e.g. head of MI5, prison governor
Self	Transformational learning Reflection and self-awareness Implementation intention Metacognitive strategies	Supplicants and recipients e.g. island dwellers under threat of sea levels rising

as part of the game outcomes, or you may be providing access to genuine information repositories like a library, or access to the internet or a virtual learning environment, and expect the students to access the information exactly as they would in a real-world situation. It depends on whether you are using the escape game to introduce a subject or to assess it, and if you want students to practice information retrieval skills as part of the game.

Knowledge required for success in the game can be:

- Explicit: students are given all of the relevant information needed within the game world.
- Assumed: students are being tested or assessed on what they already know.
- Retrievable: students use information retrieval skills to find what they need in the real world.

Knowledge needed could also be a mix of the above. In the middle of a topic, you could be consolidating learned skills and knowledge whilst moving forward to analysis and strategic thinking. You might have a puzzle where students are getting to know a foreign city – for example, Paris, France. The players are expected to read instructions in a different language on the assumption that they have all the vocabulary and grammar knowledge they need. Some of these instructions require them to use a map of the city – this is explicit knowledge given to the students as they are not expected to be familiar with Paris. Then they are left to use Google to retrieve the opening hours and entrance fees for the specific tourist attractions in the puzzle.

SETTING

'Setting' is the physical space in the game, its function and location within the story world and real world.

Sometimes the real-world setting of the game is the focus of the learning; for example, inducting students into a library or a gym, or when students are moving up a grade to a completely different institution or building. You may want the students to develop a sense of familiarity with the location and to get to know their way around. You may want the students to learn the lie of the surrounding land, whether that is an outdoor center, a campus or a town. Perhaps you want them to learn map-reading skills, or how to use the information displays and where to find them. The setting could be a place that may be seen as awe-inducing or scary, such as an interview suite, assembly stage or exam room, and you don't want the students to be disadvantaged by unfamiliarity.

Students learn best when they experience authentic learning and using the setting for what it is adds to this authenticity, as well as to the sense of immersion in the narrative.

Puzzles and learning outcomes will be around:

- Familiarization: the elements of the space and their function; including people and roles.
- Induction: basic knowledge and vocabulary of the setting and subject.
- Physical layout: the physical and/or relative locations of elements, local and micro level (this workbench).
- Real-world location: from the environs of the venue to the macro level (this planet).

Learning outcomes could include:

- The student will know the name and contact information for their subject librarian in order to get subject-specific library help.
- The student will know where to find the different artifacts, resources, and media in the library.
- The student will be able to plan a local trip using public transport.
- The student will be able to locate and name the key figures in a courtroom.

Puzzles could include:

- Eliminate suspects in a crime investigation by calculating whether they could have got to the crime scene in time from their last verified location using maps, public transport timetables, and other information sources.
- Figure out if two lecturers on campus had time to meet between lectures given the location of their classes, offices, and their timetables.
- Finding their way around a library to pick up various artifacts and drawing the route map on their library plan gives them key information for a detective narrative.
- A logic puzzle around who sat where and the direction they were facing during a trial in a courtroom.
- Identifying buildings and landmarks in the view from the windows.

Hints

The nudges are around pointing out where and how to access the information needed. The non-player characters' (NPCs) role here is to point them at the right information source, so they could be a lab assistant who could say:

> 'Have you seen this? Do you think it could be relevant?'
>
> 'Train times? I know there's a timetable around here somewhere …'
>
> 'Maybe the subject librarian would know what his favorite book was?'

Even if the setting is not important to any of your learning objectives, you need to pay attention to it. The setting of the game and the setting of the story should be as closely aligned as possible to achieve an immersive sense of presence. Making the story come alive in your venue using set dressing and props can be enjoyable and creative. However, whilst turning a classroom into an office or a secret agent headquarters (HQ) is relatively simple, Greek temples and Egyptian tombs are not so easy to pull off. You could more easily emulate an archaeological dig with a tent in the grounds, or turn a classroom into an impromptu lab and/or office for the archaeologists, using photographs, videos, 3D worlds on a computer, or even virtual reality goggles with phones to give the sense of a different place just beyond the game boundaries. This immersion is important to the authenticity of the experience and therefore to the depth of learning of the students.

If you can use a different location for the game than the regular classroom, even if it's just a different classroom, this will increase the alertness of the students as they are forced to pay attention to everything they would normally ignore. It also prevents them failing to see something you have cleverly blended into their classroom background and avoids the frustrations that this causes.

In our sample game included with the book, we use the setting of a library with learning objectives around information literacy and security concepts.

SOCIAL

'Social' refers to the interactions and collaboration between the players and with the NPCs.

Escape rooms can be good for team bonding and useful group-building exercises, where you want to create rapport swiftly in a group of people who have never met before. One reason is that the puzzles give the participants an external task focus for their communication efforts rather than relying on personal exposition. This also makes it more comfortable for neuro-diverse participants. Working in a team in the real world does not mean liking everybody in it, or knowing any personal details about them; it's about being able to communicate and cooperate. Escape rooms provide ample opportunity to demonstrate this, especially for those who normally find teamwork trying, but have gravitated towards and practiced structured social activities such as board and video games. The format is excellent for bringing to the fore all sorts of soft skills, particularly those to do with cooperation, collaboration, and communication (Cable, 2019).

So often as educators we expect our students to work in groups, or to mimic a professional team, and yet teamwork skills are a rare find within formal learning objectives. They are typically taken as a given, or as something the student simply has to learn from experience. Escape games provide this experience in a usefully compact format and provide the opportunity to raise awareness of the need to improve these skills, develop a vocabulary around them, practice them, and then use them for the situational leadership and team-player opportunities that arise with each different challenge in the game.

Given free choice, students will naturally gravitate towards their friends and people they know to make up a team for a game. The teams may be more balanced if you randomly assign players to them, or even if you deliberately mix and match students so that groups of 'usual suspects' are avoided. If you are creating a competitive game, it's especially important that the teams are seen to be made up fairly. Escape games are great group builders because everyone can focus on solving puzzles rather than social skills, so rapport is created very quickly as conversation flows around solutions – as evidenced by the noise levels rising in class. The key to success is in your puzzle design allowing everyone a moment to shine.

Puzzles and learning outcomes will be around:

- teamwork
- collaboration and cooperation
- communication skills
- personal qualities, for example courage, fairness, and empathy.

Learning outcomes could include:

- The student will use body language to reflect a positive listening attitude.
- The student will use open and closed questions appropriately to elicit relevant information.
- The student will be able to devise and communicate a set of instructions or directions.
- The student will choose to present an argument for following a particular course of action.
- The students will be able to work cooperatively in a group environment.

Puzzles could include:

- Dividing the team of players with physical barriers, so they need to communicate information to other players that they can't see.
- Creating long sequences to remember between locations or over time that need more than one person to remember correctly.
- Events occurring simultaneously that need observing or need synchronized actions from players in different locations.
- Players as a group having to elect an individual to represent them in a role-play situation or take on a specific element of a group task.

Hints

Hints are not much help when a puzzle simply requires teamwork to solve it. You can point out that they need to work together, and even perhaps as your in-game character be a part of the team, but a puzzle that requires teamwork to solve can't always have a shortcut. You may have to be obvious about what it is you want them to do, and it's preferable that you plan for this in advance by using cues alongside the puzzle rather than clues delivered as hints. The aim is for the players to solve it for themselves without hints if possible. For example, you could have graphics that illustrate what it is you want the players to do, or have a video of a previous team demonstrating what needs to be done. We've also used a lab book in one instance and a diary with a diagram in another. This can also meet additional learning objectives involving following instructions or stating the steps in a process.

In one science-themed game where the players were taking on the role of a research team who had gone missing, early in the game the players found lab coats, each with their own name badge. Later on, when there was a multi-part cooperative puzzle, the individual instruction sheets were labelled with the names of the scientists, giving a strong cue that each player had to take on a different role and complete a different task to solve the bigger puzzle.

STORY

'Story' is the narrative that leads players through the game.

Considering the role of the cast of characters in your world provides the narrative reason why the mission exists, who is giving them the clues and why they need the players to help, who the students are working for, and what your role as facilitator could be inside the storyworld. In a crime scene investigation, for example, potential NPCs include the victim of crime, the chief of police, a nosey reporter, the suspects (including the real criminal), the crime scene investigator, and so on. These characters are present in the storyworld within the artifacts that the players discover – emails, text messages, phone recordings, letters, vlogs, reports, pictures on desks, entries in diaries, and so on, as well as those roles that the facilitators take on for themselves.

The story provides an opportunity for the students to engage emotionally and ethically with the cast members of your storyworld and invest in their success, as well as the students' own successes. The students can take on a role in the world – they can all be 'investigators', or 'researchers' – or you could give individuals specific roles, and perhaps specific briefings, tools or knowledge so that the team relies on each student for a different contribution to the whole.

Inquiry-based learning encompasses a variety of pedagogical activities that center on students devising or addressing questions around real-world problems, often with a tangible outcome, and usually with a series of mini-problems to solve along the way. The small challenges involve practicing learning outcomes that are enabling objectives for more complicated higher-order thinking skills. You could think of the puzzles as demonstrating the individual enabling skills and knowledge, and the story as a chance to synthesize it all into a cohesive whole. Your game could be a summary of the skills being learned from start to finish, either as an introductory activity to a new topic or as formative or summative assessment, or revision.

Crucially, the story is where the outcome of an educational escape game can differ from a commercial room. Escape rooms end at the end of the time limit, and either you get out or you don't and that's that, the narrative just ends. This is not appropriate for an educational game when the story is part of the learning outcome. The narrative needs to be designed so that everyone gets to engage with the entire story in some way. One option is to design a timed game so that the hints are delivered on a timeframe and move players on to new challenges when the time for a specific challenge runs out to ensure success. Other routes are to write multiple endings that are equally compelling and narratively and pedagogically rewarding, or creating a different method to explore the remainder of the story when time runs out, such as an ending exposition or scripted role play. When possible, consider the opportunity to carry on with the narrative outside of the game itself during the post-game reflection to elicit creative responses from the students. Once the storyworld has been established, and the characters revealed, they can be revisited again and again to bring home the learning points. This creative response is never a part of a commercial game, yet may well be the whole reason you are creating one – to get the level of engagement that results from a deep understanding of a situation and a personal connection to its stakeholders.

An escape room can also be a fan-generated experience set in the storyworld of another author's franchise. This can be very appealing to students who are also familiar with the storyworld, and can provide the fantastical touch that's needed to get the students to step out of the mundane, and into the magic circle of play where anything can happen (Huizinga, 1955). If you are teaching a specific text, then of course you can base your narrative around it. It is up to you to decide how advantaged students are who are already familiar with the text.

Puzzles and learning outcomes will be around:

- inquiry-based learning
- problem solving
- role playing
- critical thinking.

Learning outcomes could include:

- The student will be able to grasp and summarize a complex set of plot lines.
- The student will be able to describe and scope the problem they are there to solve.
- The student will be able to detect missing information.
- The student will be able to develop a robust position, arguing their conclusions from an investigation.
- Given several individual pieces of information, the student will be able to devise a cohesive logical storyline threading through the whole.

Puzzles could include:

- Persuading the night guard to let you into the building or giving you the passcode.
- Investigating specific pieces of information amongst many, eliminating the irrelevant, to confirm they have selected the right information, for example suspects with a motive and no alibi, drug trials with certain side-effects and not others.
- Making a telephone call and having to give enough information to pass security checks, and getting the next piece of information that they need.
- Making a moral decision at the end around doing one thing or another, as a group.

Hints

Hints here can be instructions and notes left by the protagonist for the students to follow or can be dastardly teasers by some egomaniacal antagonist (like the Riddler in *Batman*).

'That guard is in a bad mood because he forgot his wife's birthday, he's going to have to make a big peace offering' [and there's chocolate in the safe].

'You need to decide one way or another, and there are only 8 minutes left!'

As well as having a good guy and a bad guy, the NPC could be a turncoat – someone who has persuaded the players to work for them in the first instance, but reveals themselves to be the bad guy halfway through whom the players have unwittingly helped with their nefarious plan. A turncoat has to be handled carefully from a hint-giving point of view and a safety point of view. The players have to be able to trust the teacher who is running the game, otherwise they will second guess and overthink anything the teacher says. Not only could this lead to them getting stuck, it could also lead to safety issues. If you are having a turncoat, make this a separate character, whether that's in person or by audio/video communications. It can also be useful to use the concept of 'turncoat' literally by wearing a specific costume piece that indicates you are playing the untrustworthy character.

In a murder mystery-themed game, intended to introduce forensic science students to the quantity, complexity and sources of information in a genuine criminal investigation, the players need to decide who committed a murder by reviewing the evidence, discovering alibis, and reading witness statements. Does the character have the motive? The means? The opportunity? Do they have an alibi? It is a process of elimination through which the players have to discover, discard, and organize large amounts of data. The evidence is found as the containers in the game are opened, the artifacts are collected, and various media is played: police interviews, the CCTV footage, and so on. When an accusation has been made, it is important that the game does not end there. There must be a pay-off for the right answer and, equally importantly, a pay-off for the wrong answer – there needs to be an ending for each suspect being accused, and a sense that the perpetrator is out there, somewhere, having got off scot-free. The story lives on.

When we used the same game to train journalists, the more evidence they uncovered, the more opportunities they got to question various witnesses at a 'live press conference,' and so gain more juicy tidbits for the news article they were to be assessed on after the game ended.

SKILLS

'Skills' refers to the discrete mastery of a specific task.

At the heart of every puzzle is a task. The puzzle is in figuring out what to do; to successfully complete any puzzle, you will always come to a stage at which you know what to do, and then you just have to do it. This task could be the demonstration of a skill.

Some commercial escape rooms have challenges based on following instructions: a superhero game that has tests of speed, reactions, and strength; a bank heist game where instructions to the players are tapped out on a hacked computer screen inside a bank vault. Some challenges rely on patrons figuring out what to do as well as how to do it – puzzle and task. Games that rely too heavily on tasks get a mixed reaction from an audience who have paid for puzzles. When used in a learning environment, however, students often relish the chance to revise their skills in this way, and you can get them to practice the same skill several times in the context of the game.

Identify a learning outcome and identify how they will demonstrate that they have met the learning outcome. Then design a puzzle where they have to perform that demonstration. Skills that are granular can be easier to define than other learning outcomes. You can have more than one skill being demonstrated to solve a puzzle, and by different members of the team (crossing over with the social dimension).

Puzzles and learning outcomes will be around:

- practice
- application
- levels of difficulty.

Learning outcomes could include:

- The student will be able to calculate the circumference of a circle using Pi.
- The student will be able to shoot an arrow to hit a target.
- The student will be able to use a spreadsheet to perform a simple calculation.
- The student will be able to search for a hashtag on social media.
- The student will be able to safely identify chemicals by scent.

Puzzles could include:

- Identifying potential witnesses in a murder mystery by their use of an event hashtag on Twitter.
- Identify which chemicals are missing from the cabinet by a combination of smell, symbol, or reagent effect.
- Using the periodic table to look up atomic weights and order elements to reveal a pattern.
- Reading a map to retrace a journey documented by landmarks and so confirm an alibi to rule out a crime suspect.

Hints

What we are doing here is testing the ability to perform a particular skill, and something about the context in which it is needed. A hint could also refer players to an in-game or external reference that explains how to perform the skill. Hints can be actual instructions which can be as general or as specific as you like, or questions that affirm the students are on the right path.

- Do you know the boiling temperature of the liquid?
- Do you think those instructions apply to this map?
- I can't ride a bike. I can't swim either. Not much help, really.

STRATEGY

'Strategy' is adopting the mode of thinking of the discipline.

Ultimately, we want students to be able to solve complex problems by bringing together a set of skills, whether those are their own skills or those of their teammates. We want them to be able to decide which skills to use and in what order for success in any situation. An escape game is a chance to practice these higher-order thinking skills. This will be both in scoping the problem using methods of inquiry aligned with the essential practices of the discipline and in solving the problem using collaboration, simulation, and skills. Sometimes this means experimenting to find out further information and that experimentation approach is a strategy. Sometimes this means different people working on different elements, or all working together. There might be limited resources in the room – calculators, torches, reference books. This explicit agreed strategy of the group to collaborate on one task is an external process, for it to work it is essential that it is articulated and discussed.

This dimension also includes cognitive strategy, which is an internal process. A simple example would be creating their own mnemonics to remember sequences of information. This development of cognitive strategies and awareness of when and how to use them is an important aspect of self-directed learning.

Once you play a few escape rooms, you will discover that there are certain types of puzzle that recur often, and that you know how to solve them. For example, players learn from repeated examples that all puzzles to open a combination padlock have two layers: one for the digits, and one for the order in which you input the digits. Knowing that this is the case leads you to be more efficient in not wasting time trying to open a padlock when you know you have only solved half of the puzzle.

When teaching students how to solve multiple-choice questions in an exam, the methodology is almost unrelated to the subject itself – there is often a throw-away answer, a trip-you-up answer, and a close-to-correct answer. Through a simple technique, a student can reduce the options in most cases to 50/50 without reference to the subject matter itself. You begin to know what you are looking for, which is very different from the stumbling around and guesswork of your first experience. At the heart of solving puzzles is completing tasks and students can become more skilled every time they practice. This is one of the ways we can use them for learning.

Puzzles and learning outcomes will be around:

- problem-based learning
- analysis and synthesis
- cognitive strategies
- handling complexity.

Learning outcomes could include:

- In conducting an investigation, the students will be able to devise a set of rules to distinguish between relevant and irrelevant information.
- The students will be able to compare two art collections, giving reasons for their positive evaluation of one over the other.
- Given a research study, the students will be able to evaluate the appropriateness of the conclusions reached based on the data presented.

Puzzles could include:

- Eliminating suspects from a murder inquiry and identifying the murderer.
- Devising an original ending to an unfinished short story.
- Judging and ranking a set of paintings by rival artists.
- Deciding which of several formulas, if any, is a safe cure for baldness.
- Writing a news story (by the deadline) using information discovered in the escape game and containing a coded message, which is accepted for publication.
- Creating a political poster to rally support for a cause.

The metapuzzle at the end of the game is an opportunity for strategic thinking. It will tie in closely with the story of the game but shouldn't be given away at the start. There is more dramatic tension and engagement when the stated mission of the game at the start is superseded in play by a more important goal. As the players go through the game, they will find and sometimes already have used artifacts that form part of the metapuzzle at the end. When the players have completed all the puzzles, they will have all the pieces they need to solve the final metapuzzle.

Hints

Each of the players should have a role in solving strategy puzzles, whether that is using specific individuals' skills to perform part of a group task, or all working together on the same thing at the same time. Hints should be around reminding the players what they have already found out, and the artifacts they have collected. They can also be around affirming or negating ideas as they come up from the players. Hints can also provide the players with a partial solution to the puzzle, so that they then need to figure out how that solution was generated, and then apply the process to the rest of the puzzle.

In 'The Locked Room', a game based on the Golden Era of Detective Fiction, the players play the role of detectives in a scenario reminiscent of Agatha Christie and Arthur Conan Doyle mysteries. The players have to decide which of the items, facts, alibis, and accounts presented are relevant, which stand up to closer inspection, and how the motives of the characters affect their potential involvement in a murder. The final meta-puzzle is to decide on the murderer, the motive, and the method, and present a convincing argument to the rest of the class. One of the learning outcomes is experiential, we want the players to 'feel' like a detective, and to understand by piecing together the evidence and rejecting what doesn't fit, how every murder mystery story is in effect a game between author and reader. The strategy of the author is to mislead and misdirect, but never cheat or deceive. The game is followed up with a task to write a detective story.

SIMULATION

'Simulation' is an approximation that takes place over time of real systems and processes.

A simulation can be identical to the real thing – such as using a spreadsheet to create a profit and loss forecast for a fictional company – or it can be a close approximation, such as using a water-filled balloon in a bladder surgery simulation, which was used in an escape game for medics. It can be a physical simulation using the actual tools or a model, or a virtual simulation using a digital environment.

Simulations will combine some of the other elements of this model and may then require players to deal with multiple types of challenges. The players may have to combine story, strategy, and skills in multiple layers to be successful at a complex challenge that simulates something that went on in history.

Puzzles and learning outcomes will be around:

- role playing
- senses and sensations
- physical constraints
- time constraints
- tools and processes.

Learning outcomes could include:

- The student will be able to use the self-service library machines to check account information.
- The student will be able to triage a patient in a set time limit.
- The student will be able to use a spreadsheet to create a profit and loss forecast.

Puzzles could include:

- Finding all the posts on social media associated with a hashtag, and then re-arranging the pictures discovered into a clue or code.
- Correctly identifying from dental records the location of tooth decay and use dental simulation equipment to drill into the correct patient's tooth to trigger a clue or code.
- Using a manual to strip down a computer/engine/sewing machine and identifying the parts to be replaced from customer records. There are further clues or codes hidden on the correct components.
- Matching chemicals to reagents by smell and symbol, with a periodic table for reference.
- Using information found on receipts that the players have to print out from a library's self-service machine.

Hints

Sometimes a simulation requires additional skills and knowledge that are in addition to the requirements of the simulated environment. For example, using software to simulate a moon landing assumes a working knowledge of how the interface controller works. If a player has not used an Xbox before, even though they may know how to perform the task in the real situation, they may be unable to perform the task in simulation using the Xbox's hand-held controller. This needs to be mitigated somehow so that players are not disadvantaged, so be explicit with the instructions on how to use the simulator, or make this the opportunity for them to learn.

In the end, if a player can't complete the simulation, and none of the players in the team can, no amount of 'hinting' will enable them to complete the task. They need to learn how to do it. That might be where a handy NPC steps in to demonstrate, either a live facilitator or a short instructional video would do. If the game is not designed for them to learn it there and then, there needs to be a way of bypassing that challenge. 'Bypassing' means allowing the players to find out the same code or clue by a completely different and valid means. It also means coming up with a narrative excuse for the players to stop what they are doing (attempting the simulation) and doing something else without feeling that they have left something undone. For example, if the players are supposed to use a precise measuring tool during a chemical experiment to capture the volume of gas produced, but aren't able to successfully use the tool and have limited materials, there could be a resource (such as a scholarly article) available in the game where the players could find the information needed.

SELF

'Self' refers to the application of attributes, qualities, attitudes, and behaviors, and reflecting about thinking.

Sometimes we want to design puzzles and activities to demonstrate attributes and qualities or to challenge current attitudes or to illuminate cognitive bias and assumptions. Some social escape rooms have at their heart an aim to change points of view and influence beliefs, such as 'The Divide' in England, which highlights the problem of homelessness. Games have a long history of being used for societal change and social justice, specifically to make players come face to face with their own attitudes and assumptions, and literally change their minds so they become a force for change themselves.

Designing some puzzles that require qualities and attributes rather than skills allows you to introduce aspects to the game that can be debriefed and reflected upon later such as patience, persistence, consistency, and courage. Sometimes the hero is the person who can be relied upon to do what might be considered boring or mundane. Sometimes the work just needs to be done, and everyone needs to muck in together, no matter how undesirable the task.

You can also create puzzles that reveal cognitive biases, helping students understand that not everyone thinks the same, and that they can change the way they think about something.

If we want a student to challenge their own thinking, we need to design an experience where their current assumptions and methods don't serve them well. The first step in designing these types of challenges is to identify the change of behavior or attitude that is needed, and think of how you can illuminate and then challenge the underlying assumptions that fuel the behavior. For example, the assumption that certain professional roles are gendered could be addressed by a logic puzzle in which both the vicar and the doctor turn out to be female.

If you are working at this level with students, then you must create plenty of time for debriefing the students and working through the experience, as well as giving them opportunity to reflect privately. It can be quite disconcerting to have long-held beliefs challenged in this way and may take a while to process. There is also opportunity in the debrief after the game to introduce concepts of metacognition, a vital part of student learning. Students need to be confident that they can learn new things, to know that they can handle both change and complexity and meet challenges head on. As A.J. Juliani (2020) puts it, 'Our job as teachers is not to prepare kids for something; our job is to help kids learn to prepare themselves for anything.' In an escape game, this means skillful facilitation and debriefing to help the students realize the transformation that has taken place, and recognize the cognitive strategies and skills they have now mastered.

Puzzles and learning outcomes will be around:

- transformational learning
- reflection and self-awareness
- implementation intention
- metacognitive strategies.

Learning outcomes could include:

- The student will demonstrate courage.
- The student will choose to work with people who they would not normally work with.
- The student will be able to articulate and implement an intention to change their behavior.
- The student will choose an appropriate cognitive strategy for learning.
- The student will have an ability and willingness to reflect on individual experiences to gain more learning from them.

Puzzles could include:

- Putting your hand in a box to feel for something.
- Reordering elements against a new value framework.
- An iterative game where the rules change up each round.
- Figuring out what assumptions someone else was working under, monitoring someone's actions or spotting someone else's mistakes, and why they made them.

Hints

The puzzle here is around why each person behaves like they do, hints are around questioning motivations, assumptions, and behavior, to encourage the students to put themselves in someone else's shoes, question their own assumptions, and think about how other people might react in different situations. This could give insights into learning styles and preferences or personality types, or how 'ethics' could mean different things to different people. The opportunity is to demonstrate and exemplify different ways of thinking.

For example, as part of a game aimed at psychology students, we wanted to introduce the idea of cognitive biases, which include functional fixedness – that is the inability to see beyond an object's primary use. At one point in the game, the challenge was to use four points on a large map to find the location where 'X marks the spot'. The trouble was there was no ruler provided to help with triangulation; instead, we provided flipchart paper, which when folded on the diagonal was long enough to help. We were delighted when one student immediately, on seeing the problem, took off her lanyard to complete the task.

Escape games give the players the chance to step out of their normal world and their normal roles and be transported to another place to play 'let's pretend'. There they apply their knowledge and skills, experience the unusual, and succeed in various challenges and tasks. We need to make sure that the learning gained is not lost or forgotten, and that we bring to the students' attention both what they achieved by applying prior learning, what they learnt during the game about the subject matter and about themselves, and get them to be intentional about how they are going to use that learning in future.

In the murder mystery game discussed earlier, one of the learning objectives was to introduce the idea of an unreliable witness, someone who unwittingly misleads the investigators by misrecalling an incident. In this case, a character provided an alibi for the murderer by saying they were together at a pub quiz on the night of the murder, when in fact although they usually attended together, that specific night the murderer didn't show up. The witness had misremembered. Later on in the game, a report on the CCTV footage by a police officer establishes that in fact the murderer had not been to the pub that evening as attested. This also provided an opportunity to talk about cognitive bias, both by the original witness who had assumed that something happened as it always had before, and potentially by the players themselves as they drew conclusions and then sought to prove themselves right, by discounting or rationalizing away anything that interfered with their original deductions.

CONCLUSION

You may not use all seven of these learning opportunities in any one game despite multiple puzzles; equally you may find that one puzzle – for example, the metapuzzle in our murder mystery example – fulfills nearly all of them. In the game that is presented with this book, the puzzles for the most part match more than one learning objective. This framework demonstrates the richness of learning opportunities that can be had from the multi-dimensional experience of an escape game.

When you are designing the game, refer to the framework and if there is an opportunity for learning, take it. The story of the game is a shared experience you can pull on multiple times in future lessons to illustrate your point or to encourage the students to recall prior learning. You can use a game to foreshadow future learning, storing that memory for later recall or application, the puzzles can introduce, demonstrate, apply, synthesize, revise, and assess topics, as well as just adding fun and perhaps a bit of silliness to your classroom.

REFERENCES

Cable, L. (2019) 'Playful interludes', in N. Whitton and A. Moseley (eds.) *Playful Learning – Events and Activities to Engage Adults*. New York: Routledge, pp. 57–70.

Huizinga, J. (1955) *Homo Ludens: A Study of the Play-element in Culture*. Boston: Beacon.

Juliani, A.J. (2020) *Learn Better*. Available online at http://ajjuliani.com/.

2
GAME SHAPES

The traditional escape room presents a locked room containing a series of challenges that a small team of players work together to solve within a specific time frame. This book presents a broader concept of 'escape games' – puzzle-based learning activities inspired by escape rooms. The room you need to escape within an hour is one possible 'game shape', but there are other shapes that can use the same concepts and the same puzzles, yet allow you more freedom to involve more students in different ways and require fewer resources. In this chapter, we explore a variety of game shapes that can be used to enable an escape game to fit into a variety of classroom settings. By starting out with a game shape in mind, it will provide constraints that will help you throughout the entire design process. With some practice, you will be able to adapt both games and puzzles to fit different class sizes and time constraints, as well as different learning outcomes.

Our assumption is that you will not be able to create a permanent escape room in your school, so the focus in this book is on game shapes that are more feasible for a classroom. This chapter focuses primarily on four game shapes:

- Pop-up escape room, which is a temporary escape room that uses the same game format as a traditional escape room but is only deployed for a short time.
- Puzzle box, where the players are working to open a series of boxes, usually played on a tabletop, instead of getting out of a room.
- Puzzle hunt, which is a paper-based series of puzzles, also usually played on a tabletop, and suitable for large groups.
- Serial stories, which breaks the escape game up into smaller chapters that are played over time instead of in one long block.

Finally, we briefly introduce hybrid models, such as megagames, to help inspire your designs to go beyond the models presented here and digital tools that can be used to implement any of these shapes. This is a chapter that you can read now to get an idea of the game shapes appropriate for your classroom situation, and then return to as you start to create your game for more detailed advice.

POP-UP ESCAPE ROOM

ADVANTAGES

- Close to an immersive commercial escape room experience.
- Good when simulating elements of the environment for learning outcomes.
- Easy integration of a human actor.

DISADVANTAGES

- Small team size makes this unfeasible for the only in-class activity for a larger class.
- High resource cost, both in equipment and human engagement as a game master (GM) or actor.

A pop-up escape room takes place in a specific venue and is a time-constrained game for one team to play at a time. Like a commercial escape room, the game is designed to be run multiple times with different teams, perhaps having one classroom reserved for the escape room for a week. Pop-up escape rooms tend to use the same types of puzzles, challenges, and locks as a traditional escape room, but the environment is much less detailed. The props are portable and less expensive than in a permanent room, as they don't need to be robust to handle thousands of plays. They may be set up to run continuously for a week or designed to be deployed for a few hours a day and then taken down. They may use desk drawers, storage closets, lockers, or other furnishings that already exist in the space.

As you will most likely be using an office, the corner of a library, a storage room or classroom that is not in use, it can help your immersion to consider building the game concepts around that space. What are the fixtures, fittings, and features of the venue that can be incorporated into the story and puzzle design? If it is a bland classroom, then turning it into an office or a lab might be your best bet, but if you get access to the school chapel or the porter's lodge, or other special location, especially one with some history, then you should incorporate the setting into the story. It's too good an opportunity for immersion. If you are in a dining room, replace the menus and specials board with versions that incorporate puzzle elements, but at first glance appear to be part of the room. What unusual venues could you use? A cricket pavilion or locker room? Backstage in the school hall? The eco-garden?

Consider too who the other users of the building are, and what role you can give them in the game. In one biopiracy-themed game set in a greenhouse in a public botanical garden, part of the game story is that the players have to hide from any passing members of the public who might 'report' them for breaking into an out-of-bounds area. Although this (probably) won't happen, the facilitator/game master/helpful agent can make the players hide when there's a chance of being spotted. Along those lines, it is important to ensure security officers and school administration be warned of any unusual behavior that may be taking place as part of the game, and that you undergo appropriate risk assessment for any physical hazards.

Locked containers in a pop-up room are more than likely going to be mobile boxes, as it is unlikely that you will be able to add a hasp and staple for a padlock to any of the furniture. Sometimes, drawers and desks are lockable and the keys can be useful for gating access to subsequent puzzles, but it's risky to make searching for keys part of the game. It's too hit and miss, can lead to frustration, doesn't teach anything, and can end up causing a disaster if the key goes missing. There may be a way to use existing handles, zip ties, ropes, chains, and padlocks in a creative way to block entry to a drawer instead of using a built-in lock. Another concept is to mimic the structure of an escape room by putting lockable containers inside desk drawers, and then some of these containers hold information and a smaller padlocked box. This provides a game model that feels like an escape room, but remains portable.

There may well be elements of the room that you don't want the players to touch, or they physically can't touch, but you do want to use in your game. Is there a display case, pictures on the wall, or bookshelves? Is there a computer or a TV and a video player? Puzzles that use floor plans of the room, transparent overlays, silhouettes, or photos/videos of existing room elements can work really well and make the game feel like it belongs in that location.

In a pop-up escape room, you generally can't fix anything to a surface as you must leave the venue as you found it. When you visit a venue with a view to converting it into an escape room, make a note of the number of pictures you can take down or replace and what picture hooks remain for you to use. Do you need to cover any surfaces with cloth? What is the view from the window like, and is there anything there you can incorporate into a puzzle? What breakable objects or trip hazards need to be removed from the room for the safety of players rushing around? Are there enough surfaces for you to put your props, containers, and puzzles on, and somewhere for the players to use as their working surface? What can be moved out of the space and what must stay?

For a modern setting, 'magic' flipchart paper that electrostatically attaches to the wall (and is reusable) can be covered with formulae and diagrams to create a scientist's office or lab, or a secret agent briefing room, out of any location. You can also use it to disguise red reveals (where you look through red translucent plastic at a message to see the non-red letters) and ultraviolet (UV) ink as part of your puzzle-making. It is important when writing on a whiteboard surface to be aware that some players accidentally (or on purpose) erase whiteboards, so using a temporary surface and a permanent marker can solve that problem.

As it is harder to have puzzle elements in the room if you can't affix them to anything, sometimes incorporating digital elements is a way around this restriction. If the venue has a website, or social media accounts, they might be amenable to some temporary adjustments whilst the game is running, or you could create fake sites and accounts just for the game. If you are going to be running several games, then it's worth investing in online assets that belong to your storyworld and its corporations, communities and characters. The players could use online research skills to find out real information about the location or organization, or you could set up fictional accounts, or straight-up puzzles that are accessed via Quick Response (QR) codes found around the room. By combining the digital with the physical, more puzzles can be made and gated than are possible within the constraints of the venue.

PUZZLE BOX

ADVANTAGES

- Can be used with small groups or adapted for a classroom with multiple copies/stations.
- Low requirements for an environment mean that it's less expensive than a full room.
- Portable and can work well in a classroom environment.
- If designed appropriately, can be run completely on its own without the need for the facilitator to interact with the game.

DISADVANTAGES

- May require many copies of the same materials for all groups.
- Physical immersion and emotional engagement are less likely.
- Helping many groups at the same time can be overwhelming for one teacher without some type of self-help hint system.
- Role-playing challenges are difficult to implement with a high number of groups.

The puzzle box shape is based on the idea of players trying to break into a box, or series of boxes, instead of trying to break out of a room. A regular-sized class can be broken into teams, and each team has their own mini tabletop escape game or puzzle box to unlock and solve. Players start with challenges and one or more locked boxes, and upon solving a challenge, can open one box, which then leads to more challenges and additional locked containers. The containers can fit inside each other, or you can have several locks visible at once, some or all of which must be opened to continue. It's good practice to only have one of each type of lock visible at once or to have the locks labeled in some way, so when the players get a code, it is clear which lock they have to open. Good design is about having the thing that is difficult in the room be the challenge that is intended, which is not figuring out which of five four-digit locks is opened with a specific code.

The puzzle box concept for classrooms was made popular in the United States through Breakout EDU (http://breakoutedu.com). When it started, Breakout EDU was presented as an open source platform for teachers to use to create escape games for classrooms. They sold a Breakout EDU kit with boxes, locks, and other accessories, but also listed out everything so that teachers could build their own kit. They created a database of games, where they contributed some games and allowed teachers to upload games to share with others, and it was an open-source collaborative space where people were creating and sharing. The concept was that teachers could get a Breakout EDU kit (or just buy the components), and then the games were designed to be printed out and played with the kit.

Then the company model changed, and they no longer presented themselves as open source. They built up a Breakout EDU platform and charged an annual fee for access to the platform, which contained tools for running a digital version of a Breakout EDU game. They designed more games that were behind this paywall. They still have a Free Breakout EDU account option, which will allow anyone to access the games that were designed under the open source concept, so not everything requires users to pay. But the tone of the Breakout EDU space has changed from its open-source roots to a more privatized model to support a staff and the professional development of games.

One of the biggest impacts that Breakout EDU has had on puzzle boxes is the incorporation of a hasp, which allows the designer to put multiple locks on a box (see Figure 2.1).

The hasp leads to a design model where the players get the materials for many puzzles at once, and each puzzle then opens a lock on the hasp. This creates a situation where the team can split up and work on different challenges at the same time. However, if the goal is that each player is working toward the same learning outcomes, using a non-linear model where the players can split up can create the situation where not every player gets to engage with every challenge. Splitting up is fine for a recreational escape room, where the goal is to solve the puzzles quickly, but if your goal is to have everyone working on every challenge, then the game needs to be designed so that the challenges are linear (or that every challenge done by a split team conveys the learning outcome).

The process of designing for a puzzle box is similar to designing for an escape room. The basic structure is that each of the challenges in the game will lead the players to

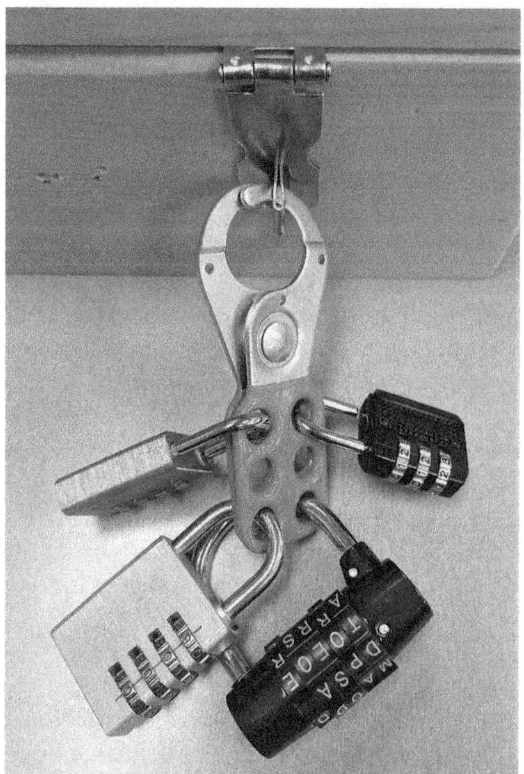

Figure 2.1 Hasp with padlocks

opening a locked container, which then gives them their next challenge. This structure can be made more complicated by giving the players more than one challenge at once, creating moments of non-linearity in the game flow. By nesting multiple boxes inside a large box, the designer gains significant freedom in how to structure their puzzles. The example in Figure 2.2 shows graphically how a puzzle box with one large locked box that contains two smaller locked boxes, each of which has an additional locked box, allows the designer a variety of ways to convey their narrative through different gating and game flow.

If there isn't the budget to have boxes and locks for each team, Breakout EDU's concept of the 'lock parking lot' can be used (www.breakoutedu.com/locks). The idea is that the teacher has one of each lock on their desk. The students figure out the code that they wish to try in a lock and write down their guess. They can then come up and try out the lock to see if it opens. If they open the lock, then the teacher will give them what they found inside. It's not as exciting as having a locked box, but it greatly reduces the tendency for players to simply try different combinations in the lock to try

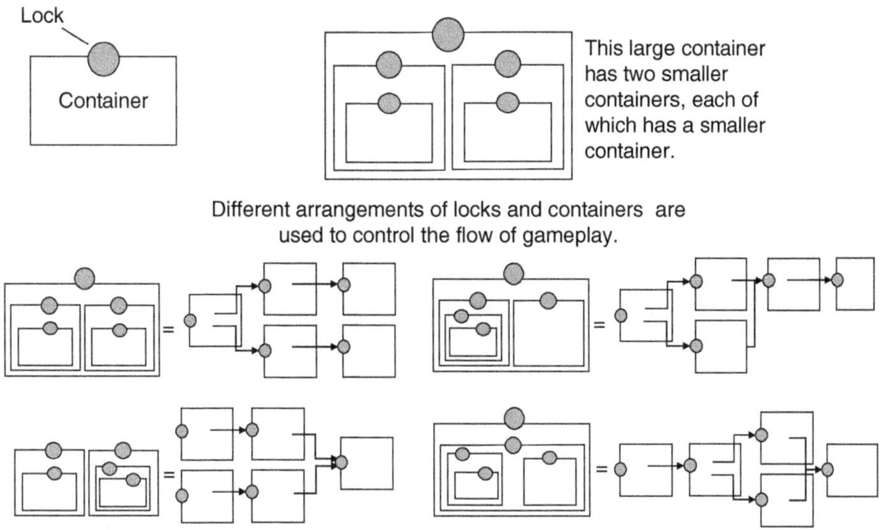

Figure 2.2 Different methods of nesting containers

to get it open without solving the puzzles. Having the students write down their guess first prevents students from just coming up and trying many different combinations.

Another design practice to avoid is repurposing classroom worksheets to lead to an answer for a lock. Using the same worksheets that you might use in a traditional class, but then checking for the right answer with a physical or digital lock, will engage students slightly more the first few times. As the real-life affordances of a puzzle box are so much greater than doing a pencil-and-paper worksheet, we encourage teachers to think beyond the worksheet and create challenges that could not be done in a traditional classroom at desks. It's a waste of an activity day to spend the money and time to make a 'game' where the students are simply doing what they would normally do in the classroom, but they are checking their answer with a padlock.

The padlocks that are visible are a hint as to what sort of answer is needed, so much so, that some players start by grabbing a lock that requires a word and seeing what relevant words they can spell – so 'Santa' is not a good choice for a Christmas game. First-time players will often sit with a wordlock and include it in their puzzle solving, thinking that the very order of the letters on a padlock, or the number of each letter, will somehow help them solve it. For the same reason, three-digit padlocks are not recommended because they can be bruted in a matter of minutes. ('Bruted' refers to a lock or puzzle being solved with brute force rather than logic. This doesn't mean breaking the padlock, just that the physical constraints of three dials and ten digits are used to guess the code by sequentially trying every possible combination.)

A puzzle box does not need to only use the items that are included in the box. As the puzzle box will be played in a classroom, elements in the classroom can also be introduced to the game. Putting up displays or posters, or hiding things 'in plain sight' can add a searching element to a puzzle box, and get learners up and out of their seats. If each group has their own box, then you need to ensure that one team's searching doesn't ruin the game for another team. The common solution to this is to have posters or items that are in a part of the classroom hidden from the rest of the room, so that teams can observe without disturbing things. Another solution is to have multiple copies of the item, so that when one team claims something, it can be replaced. Doing this in an area of the class where other students can't see will ensure there is still some mystery.

When running tabletop games for many teams at once, consider removing the chairs from around the tables, before the students come in. This raises the energy in the room, encourages them to walk around, and as each team clusters around their table, their backs create a natural screen so that other players can't take a peep at their solutions.

THE ONE-BOX WONDER

A cheaper version of an escape game can be played with just one box and one four-digit padlock per team - ideal if you suffer from budget constraints. The game has five puzzles, one for each of the digits of the code, and one puzzle to convey the order of inputting the digits.

Each of four puzzles is color-coded with a colored border. These puzzles all solve to give a different digit. A fifth puzzle conveys colors and the numbers one, two, three, and four. For example, the fifth puzzle could consist of ten book covers, each with a border around them, so that one book has a red border, two have a green, three have a yellow, and four have a blue border. This gives the order red, green, yellow, blue, which is the order that the color-coded puzzle solutions needed to be in to open the padlock (see Figure 2.3).

The puzzle works the same whether you have all ten books and borders printed side by side on one sheet of paper, or you have each book on a separate sheet. However, the latter gives more opportunity for more of the players to work on it at once. Every team member can be working on this at the same time, which is perfect for the final puzzle. Although it's simple, it can take a while to solve. Depending on how much information you have on the book covers, the players will look at anything other than the border, especially when they have not solved any of the other puzzles yet. They will try inputting every number they can see to start with, so try to avoid having any numbers on the book covers and you'll stop some of their frustration. Also avoid colors if you can.

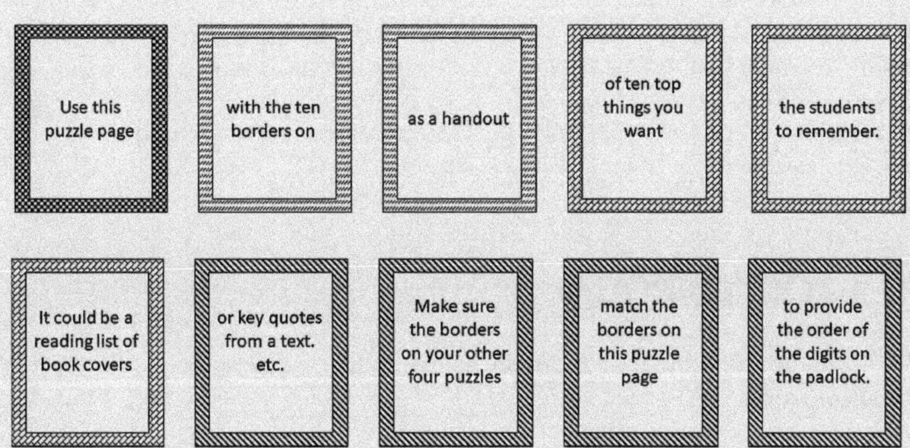

Figure 2.3 The 'border order' puzzle for the One-Box Wonder

As you need to have all the puzzles out at once, the color-coding also helps the players understand which parts, props, and papers go together. However, you don't have to have all the parts of each puzzle on the table. You could use posters on the walls, or label items in the classroom or lab, and have the students walking around to discover these elements. Just make sure they are color-coded or otherwise strongly visually linked to the puzzle elements on the table.

This game design is interesting to discuss with the players after the game. On paper, the design looks like a good collaborative game, but because all five puzzles are visible at once, it's easy for the players to split up and take a puzzle each without collaborating at all. The lack of formative feedback is also an issue. All the puzzles have to be solved to open the padlock, which means you can't discover if you've just got one right. Brute forcing of the final one or two digits once the color-coding has been cracked is a common tactic, and can lead to a discussion on whether it's fair or not to miss or bypass one or two puzzles in this way.

'Stations' or round robin

If you have a large class, a reasonable amount of kit, but not enough to create several duplicate tabletop games, you could create a series of stations. There are several ways to facilitate this, based upon the number of groups in the room. If there are a number of groups equal to the number of stations, then players take it in turns to play each station. Each station can be a mini-escape game or just one puzzle (or task) on each station, and each is complete in itself. All stations need to take the same amount of time to solve, as all teams are moved on to the next stations at the same time. Teams may fail to solve a station, but still get to move on to the next station with a clean slate and start again. The stations need to be reset between teams, so making the stations easy for teams to reset is important. You'll find that no matter where they start in the room, the teams will get faster with each station.

THE LOCKED ROOM

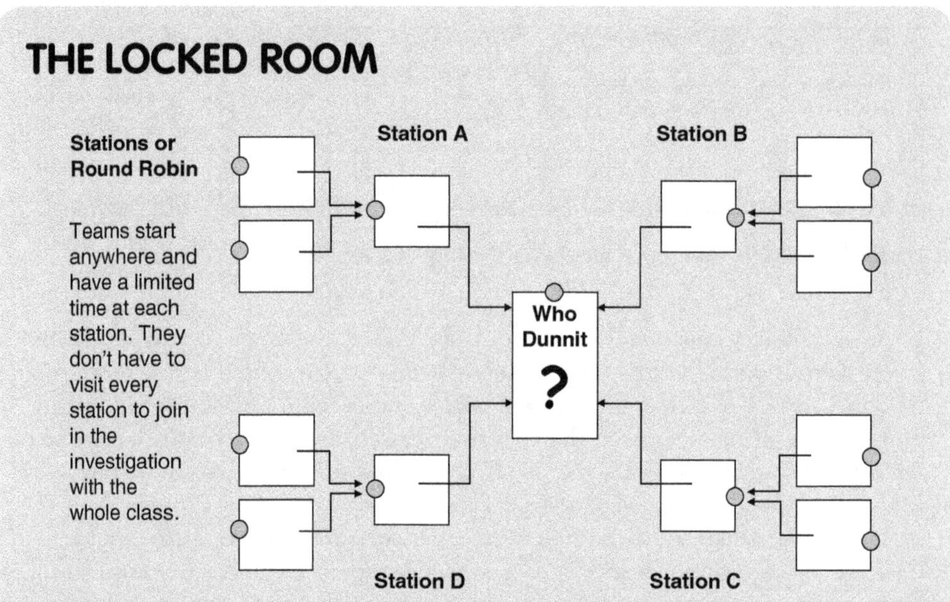

Figure 2.4 The stations game format for The Locked Room

Figure 2.4 shows the game format for The Locked Room, which was designed to introduce the detective genre to an English class. Taking inspiration from 'The Murders in the Rue Morgue' by Edgar Allan Poe, which was the first ever detective story, and from Arthur Conan Doyle and Agatha Christie, the idea was to get the students solving the case in the same way that the reader solves the case in detective fiction. We created a traditional Manor House Mystery where the Lord of the Manor is found dead (optionally in a room that has been locked from the inside). Each of the suspects – the second wife, the nanny, the first son, and the butler – has their own room in the house represented by a table, with puzzles themed appropriately. On each table, there are three boxes. The players are told that they have enough information given on each table to open the first two boxes and opening those boxes will reveal the information they need to open the third box.

In each box, in addition, there is a piece of evidence that will be useful in solving the overall metapuzzle mystery.

To save duplicating the evidence for each team, the players are asked instead to make notes and take photographs, before they are locked away again for the next team to try to find. The faster they are, the more time they have to examine the evidence they've found. At the end of the game, each group has to make their argument for whodunnit, before which there is some evidence swapping between teams to make sure everyone has the full story.

Note that you can design a stations game where each group only gets to play a subset of the tabletop games. This leads to a discussion round that involves the students telling each other what they found, and what their conclusions are from it. Playing a game like this at the start of a term or class can get the students into lively discussion, which can then be held up as the exemplar for later classes where you want the discussion but don't have the game. You can use this concept to bring about a learning outcome where you want students to understand that there are different perspectives on a topic; by having each team do activities that are similar, but with a different narrative perspective, it can lead to an enlightening debriefing afterwards.

A different approach to the stations model is to have packets with challenges at each team's table, and as the players solve one challenge, they can then go to a station to see if their answer will open it. They are then instructed to take one item from the container and return to their table to work on their next challenge. One possible design problem with this model is that the team has access to many puzzles at once and can be overwhelmed. A solution to this is to have the packets with the challenges at each station. The team sends one member to a station who collects a packet. The team works on the challenge at their home table until they have a solution, then return to that station with the answer. Each locked container provides part of the metapuzzle, which the team can solve after they have visited all of the containers.

PUZZLE HUNT

ADVANTAGES

- Handles a large group of players well.
- If most challenges are pencil and paper, the resource cost is low and can accommodate many groups of players.
- There are several free online tools that facilitate this kind of game.

DISADVANTAGES

- Some types of physical challenges aren't feasible.
- The game is, in general, less immersive than games that use physical components.
- Without a hint and answer system in place, it can be overwhelming to facilitate.

If boxes and locks require too many resources, then a puzzle-hunt model can bring about a similar experience but with much less overhead, as they are primarily paper-based games that can handle many groups or teams at once. While puzzle-hunt teams start at a table as their 'home base', they may have challenges that require them to travel to different areas, to observe, to explore, or to even play a mini-escape room. While the types of challenges that you are creating for classroom-based games are simpler than most puzzle-hunt puzzles, the overall structure is useful.

The typical structure of a puzzle hunt starts by providing teams with a set of puzzles. Each puzzle usually has two tasks – a larger process-based task, and then a more conceptual 'aha'-based realization where the entire puzzle resolves into a single word or phrase. A simple example would have students taking individual words on cards and rearranging the cards to complete three quotes, but the answer that is needed is the character in a play who said all of these quotes. Each of these answer words then feed into a larger metapuzzle, which will be the gate to let the players continue on to another set of puzzles. After the players finish a metapuzzle, they submit their answer to a game master who will then give them the next packet of puzzles. We have structured some of our sample game using a puzzle-hunt format, as players get a packet of three puzzles, then complete a metapuzzle, then get another packet with two challenges, and finally a packet with a role-playing and reflective challenge.

The goal of a recreational puzzle hunt is to unlock the metapuzzles as quickly as possible to finish first, so the approach that puzzle-hunt teams take is different than you want your students to take in your escape games. In a puzzle hunt, the teams will only solve as much of a puzzle as they need to in order to get the answer, and they will attempt to figure out the metapuzzle with as little information as possible. This is the impact of the 'race' structure – it encourages reaching the goal over exploring the challenges. Some puzzle hunts require teams to complete each puzzle as well as the metapuzzle, which creates the strategy of 'backsolving'. Backsolving is where you figure out the metapuzzle early, get the answer words to the individual puzzles, and then work those puzzles backwards using the answer as a guide. If a set of puzzles all contribute words that make a phrase, figuring out some of the puzzles and then guessing at the missing words in the phrase may allow players to skip out on puzzles.

As you have developed challenges around learning outcomes, you don't want students skipping puzzles to focus on just getting answer words and solving the metapuzzle. This is akin to students spinning the dials on a lock to find the right answer. To prevent this, the designer of the puzzle has to consider how to add obfuscation into the puzzle so that the path to solve is not clear for someone starting with the solution. For example, in The Locked Room game above where the students unscrambled three quotes all referring to the same character, the students could come up with the answer after finding just one quote. To add obfuscation, you can add another layer to the challenge, where each of three quotes from a play is said by a different person, but the answer is the common friend that each of these characters have. Therefore, only getting one quote and one person who said that quote isn't enough to figure out the answer.

If you have developed a game where backsolving is possible, it can be useful to have a pre-game discussion with the students to help them understand that this game is not just about solving it quickly, but going through the process of solving it. This is also a lesson in structuring the game – the more emphasis you put on 'being the fastest team', the more you encourage players to 'win at all costs'. We recommend you do not reward being the first team to solve the puzzles, as this encourages racing to the end over going through the process.

There are tools from the puzzle-hunt community that can be useful in facilitating a large group. A free tool that is commonly used is Google Forms, where you can create checks on the answers that players enter into the form, which can then lead students to additional parts of the form. You can then integrate media into the form. One of the top commercial tools at the time of writing this book is ClueKeeper (http://cluekeeper.com), which is an app that automates the delivery of hints and checking the answers. While ClueKeeper is not free to use, it does have some free puzzle hunts that you can participate in to get an idea of how it works. ActionBound (http://actionbound.com) is a free game creator that incorporates location-based mobile gaming, QR codes, physical challenges, and quizzes; it also has an educational license if you want your students to create their own games. Scanova (http://scanova.com) has a 14-day free trial which also gives you storage for any elements that your QR codes point to – so no need for a website even, or hosting costs. Your institution or library may also have licenses to similar tools that you could use for your escape game creation.

Puzzle hunts typically also involve some physical activities where the players leave the table. They may be instructed to find something in the setting of the room or that is hidden in another space and observe it for information needed to solve the puzzle. In the sample game at the end of this book, one way to incorporate an observational puzzle is to create posters out of the charts for the 'Graph Grifting' challenge (Challenge 1c) and put them up around the room. Rather than create something for your game, you could instead use a permanent display or statue as part of your game. In creating game shapes for large numbers of players, you can mix and match the activities. You could use a digital large-scale game or puzzle hunt to keep the bulk of the players occupied, whilst in smaller groups, they take turns to complete a small physical escape game.

THE ENVELOPE GAME

I was challenged to create the cheapest escape game ever and responded with a game based on spoken passwords. In this game, each team was given a number of envelopes with a passphrase on the front, which they were told to hide about their person until a player from another team approached them and said the correct passphrase.

Getting the envelope back to your teammates and ripping it open to start on the next puzzle turned out to be as satisfying as opening a box, especially as you had to first wrest it from the reluctant hands of a competing player. It was also gratifying in that moment to see where the other team was with their game, and this added to the sense of competition in the room.

This game has to be written with a set number of teams in mind, so that in a three-team game, team A has team B's envelopes, team B has team C's envelopes, and team C has team A's envelopes. Once written, you will need to make the teams shrink and grow depending on the number of players, rather than reducing or increasing the number of teams if you have fewer or more players than you were expecting. You will need to write isomorphic puzzles, so that the puzzles are all solved the same way and the learning point is the same, but the players can't look at another team's answers (on their envelopes), and therefore bypass their own puzzles. It is important with a game like this to have a discussion about fair play, as the game could break down if players decide not to be honest about handing over an envelope or misunderstand how that part of the game works.

SERIAL STORY

ADVANTAGES

- By only using a small amount of time each week, it is easier to fit into a classroom schedule.
- Can be changed week by week to adjust to the students' performance.
- Less overwhelming to get started with, as the teacher can learn from design mistakes and improve future weeks.

DISADVANTAGES

- Earlier content is forgotten if debriefing only occurs at the end of the game.
- Will take more time overall, as the setup and narrative will need to be repeated each week to get the players into the game.

Serial stories are games that take place over a longer period of time, where the players are immersed for shorter periods of time, but on a more regular basis. For example, students may start each day of class for two weeks with a 20-minute activity, or the game may be a pervasive game that continues over a semester. These episodic games can be any of the aforementioned models – mini-escape rooms, locked boxes, paper challenges, or other sorts of activities such as physical simulations or role-playing activities.

Conceptually, each session should be a self-contained episode. The start will be reminding the players about the story thus far (or asking them to report to the class what has happened). Then, the challenge for the day is introduced. After the players have worked through the challenge, there is a debriefing of what went on, to help connect the activities to the learning outcomes. It can be fun to end with a discussion of what could happen next (and this might give the instructor some good ideas for surprises for next time).

Having different types of activities for each week will create a more exciting game experience for players, as there will be anticipation each week about what will happen the next week. This also can be a good experience for someone new to creating these games, as the stakes are lower for a week's activity; if something doesn't work, then having a good debriefing about what went wrong and tying that into the learning outcome can be just as valuable as having a successful game. Having a ten-minute game fall apart is much less costly to valuable class time than having an hour-long game fall apart in the first ten minutes.

While the entire 'season' of the serial stories does not need to be developed before starting, it is useful to have an idea about where the story will go, and how the story will connect to the learning outcomes. That said, it is also beneficial to have some flexibility, so that you can change the games to be responsive to the players. Much like a game master preparing a tabletop role-playing game from week to week, you can allow some of the players' predictions to come true in the narrative.

The serial story framework is also useful as a creation assignment. For the first few weeks, you create the story and the challenges, but then you allow groups of students to develop the challenges for future weeks of class. It is recommended that you review their plans before having the entire class play the challenge, as this will allow you to ensure the narrative and challenge are appropriate, but this type of co-created puzzle game can be quite engaging for a class.

Serial stories are also useful when you are modeling something that pans out over time like the launch of a new business or the stages of testing a drug or are tracking something that happens in real life – for example, the baseball season or the Tour de France. Whether it's real or fictional you can take inspiration from real life events, trending topics, and news items to incorporate them into your story as you go along.

HYBRID GAMES

ADVANTAGES

- Easier to design, as the format of the game can change for the needs of the narrative and learning outcomes.
- Can handle people better, as bottlenecking issues can be solved by using a different style of challenge at those points.

DISADVANTAGES

- Requires the designer to be comfortable creating different types of challenges.
- Can be difficult to test without a large group to identify bottlenecks.
- May be overwhelming to players who aren't comfortable learning multiple types of challenges in one game.

If you have huge numbers of students, you may want to consider creating a hybrid game that takes in some of the elements of all these game shapes and styles to provide the players with a game experience that matches their engagement with it. You could create a pen and paper treasure hunt, or a location-based mobile game where one of the challenges is a 15-minute tabletop escape game – and you have enough tabletop games for several, but not all, teams to complete at once. Or you might have each team pick up a briefcase they have to solve a puzzle to get into, and that then contains further puzzles and clues.

If you have a large class and a traditional escape room, you have to plan for the teams to play at different times, which means finding an activity to occupy the rest of the class each time the game is played. Having a short escape room as just one of the activities in a puzzle hunt can work if you build in time for each team to play the mini-escape room. Note that setting up this mini-escape room as the end activity will lead to a bottleneck, as frustrated players are waiting their turn, having finished everything else. It's better to have the game be played in the middle of the game while there are other activities to solve so that you can avoid this end-of-game bottleneck, or provide set times for each group to do the escape game, and they work the rest of the game around those timings.

Every team does not have to be able to do every challenge, some will be time-limited, some will be limited by resources. Maybe you don't even get to know about the mini-escape room on campus until you have solved a certain set of puzzles, which some teams may not even attempt. Don't worry about giving everyone the same experience – that will never happen – instead, think about how to give everyone the opportunity, and how to manage expectations – like saying at the start some of the challenges will be time-limited.

There are various factors that you can change, or adapt the game to, which will create permutations you can use for different purposes. The shape of the game will be determined by the number of players, the time allocated, the locations, and whether teams play all at the same time or at different times, and whether they are able to interact with each other or not during the game. You can even have games where two or more teams are competing, but have to cooperate at certain points.

Mega-Escape Game

A mega-escape game is a game involving different classrooms all in the same narrative world. For example, there could be a large bomb, requiring students in computer classes to work on the programming and wiring of the bomb, students in a psychology class to engage with the people who planted the bomb, students in a chemistry class to figure out what combination of materials will be needed to defuse the bomb, and students in a journalism class to document everything.

Players start at a home game, but all the games are different, and have different puzzle components on them. These games can be very complex as the players are opening locks on boxes to collect puzzle parts and information, but may end up trading the parts of one puzzle with other teams to enable them to collect all the elements they need to open another puzzle. In the above example, the psychology game may reveal that the people who made the bomb did so in a battery factory, which will provide information about the potential chemicals used to the students in the chemistry game.

If you are running a large game for hundreds perhaps, say for induction, you'll need a room (or set of staffed rooms) large enough to hold everyone for the briefing, and then a single room big enough to bring everyone back together for an 'awards ceremony' at the end. If you can incorporate photo challenges into your game, this makes for a great slide show. My favorite photo challenges are getting teams to film a secret handshake and submit it via the right hashtag on social media, and an espionage task of getting them to secretly photograph or film another team without that team being aware, and emailing it in. These are always great fun to reveal during the awards ceremony.

MAKING IT 'VIRTUAL'

While all of these examples are based upon players engaging with games in the physical world, it is possible to adapt any of these concepts to games that can be played at a distance. While virtual reality (VR) technology is a possibility for an escape room, we recognize that most teachers don't have the time or resources to create VR puzzle-based games. Instead, there are easy methods to take a physical game and adapt it so it can be played at a distance. Videoconferencing tools can allow the students to engage with the instructor and other students, and to view physical puzzles via a video feed. During the time of the COVID-19 pandemic, many recreational escape rooms offered remote play experiences so teams could work with someone in the room who had a camera and provided them instructions. The narrative could be developed around this concept, where the players are advisors who are instructing someone 'in the field' who is engaging with the physical challenges.

Another route that many educators are taking to create digital puzzle-based escape games is through the use of Google Forms. Students can be provided with the image of a puzzle or a PDF to print out, and then enter the answer into a Google Form. The creator can add validation to the fields in the Google Form, and direct the players to different screens based upon the answers they enter or choose. This same concept can be used with Google Slides or PowerPoint to create an interactive slide show, where players are shown an image, and then click on their guess on the screen. Hotspots on the screen can then be tied to other pages in the slide show.

Breakout EDU has made the 'digital breakout' popular. In these digital games, the boxes are replaced by websites or apps. The players work through a challenge on paper or on the PC/tablet, and then take that solution and put it into a website or app, which will then give them their next direction. The Breakout EDU Digital platform has many digital games ready for instructors to use, and also has created tools to allow teachers and students to create their own digital breakouts. Escape-team (escape-team.com) is a free app that mimics different styles of padlocks.

A simple approach to making games digital is through a series of password-protected documents. The players are given a series of files, only one of which can be opened at the start. When they solve the challenge in that file, they get a password, which they can then use to open the next file. Using a free tool such as WordPress (www.wordpress.com), you can create a series of blogposts with every kind of media, but password protected. Or you could create a series of WordPress websites based in your fictional world, each of which contains information to help with the quest, and can have password-protected gates to further information.

Opting for the digital version of an escape game can have a significant downside, and that is a potential loss of player-to-player engagement. When someone is engaging with a screen, their attention moves out of the real world and into the screen world. We have been trained to shut out the real world when focusing on the screen, so the purely digital games have a good chance of losing the 'magic' of their real-world counterparts.

There are some activities that make sense for using digital resources, such as research using online sources. Our recommendation would be to minimize the non-essential digital moments, or design them in a way that requires real-world collaboration to solve. For example, you could have several QR codes that lead to parts of an online picture that needs putting together by the players using their phones like pieces of a jigsaw puzzle to see the whole image. Recreational apps such as Space Team (https://spaceteam.ca/) and Tick-Tock (www.ticktockthegame.com/) show how cooperation can take place between digital platforms and across geographical distance. Learners enjoy telling stories about how they solved puzzles, and sharing what they have found out, so you can make this collaboration one of the rounds or challenges in the game.

There are many more complex ways to create digital puzzle-based games. For something more focused on branching narratives, Twine (www.twinery.org) is a free online tool that makes it easy to create a choose-your-own adventure – you can even create combination checkers with it. Aris (https://fielddaylab.org/make/aris/) is a free educational tool that allows you to build an interactive story, tour or game. Players can complete quests, collect items, and talk to virtual characters in augmented reality using their phones in location-based mobile games.

It is beyond the scope of this book to explore how to make these born-digital games, but many of the concepts presented here will be useful if you decide to explore digital game development.

3
WORLD DESIGN

This chapter leads the reader through the process of creating a consistent world in which the game will be set, developing the roles for the players, thinking about their allies and opponents, and developing the realities of the world from both the players' perspective and the place in which the game is set.

A key difference between a puzzle-based escape game for education and puzzles used in the classroom is the narrative structure that brings the puzzles together. A commercial escape room is designed to entertain, even to shock or scare, but in the classroom we want to educate. Whilst skills and knowledge can be applied at the puzzle level, the narrative gives us the opportunity for learning. To develop this narrative structure, the first step is to create the world in which the narrative makes sense. This world consists of the geographical location of the players and puzzles, the timeframe in which the narrative is set, the specific space where the narrative takes place, the roles and goals of players within this space, and the roles and goals of the allies and opponents within the space. A layer on top of this to be considered throughout is the genre or overall feeling of the game. Along the way, each of these elements are opportunities to connect the players to the learning outcomes, so this should always be taken into account with every decision. During this chapter, each of these elements are explored in order to help you create a cohesive narrative where the players feel like a part of the world.

Before we start this world-building exploration, it is important to recognize that much of this content will not be presented directly to the players. It can be tempting to present everything up front to the players as you worked hard to develop it, but that will be overwhelming. World-building is background work that ensures the puzzles and narrative that you create later are consistent. Players can develop expectations as to how to engage with your challenges if you are building everything in a consistent world.

LIZ'S STORYWORLD

I use the same storyworld in all my modern-day games. To bring the organizations I create to life within the game world, each entity needs to have their own logo, tagline, branding, etc. like the Acme Corporation in the Road Runner cartoons. Rather than recreate this every time, I have a couple of competing research companies and a university in my storyworld. All my characters have something to do with one or more of these entities. The researcher who invented time travel (sadly, only one-way) shared a university flat with the doctor who accidentally created the zombie plague whilst researching age-reversing cosmetics. As a creator, I have a lot of fun making up the backstories, but it also saves so much time with making props - like branding internal memos or the local newspaper - and it keeps the storyworld, the timelines, and me consistent.

Bearing in mind the players always save the day in 60 minutes or so, the storyworld naturally resets itself to neutral between games. I can invent time travel in the same world that I have a zombie plague, and everyone still gets home in time for tea.

Currently, the storyworld has two rival mega-corporations: Mobius Inc, which is a bio-tech company, and The Tinman Group, which specializes in robotics and AI. I also created the UK Space Initiative (USI) and the British Unidentified Flying Object Society (BUFOS) for an alien abduction themed game. The University of Northern England is where the boffins who are running all these research projects and organizations graduated from, and they all have personal history with each other, stole each other's partners, that sort of thing. A lot of the personal drama isn't used particularly heavily in game, but it can be played up or down as needed. The scenes of crime officers tend to concentrate on the mechanics of the murder in 'The Case of the Overstayed Welcome', whereas the journalists are keen to uncover secret love affairs and blackmail subplots amongst the cast of characters.

Creating these organizations and characters are enjoyable branding and creative writing exercises for students, and it's very rewarding for them to 'meet' their own creations in the game. Invite students to write the scripts and film the mission briefs too.

STARTING WITH THE GENRE

The first decision facing a designer of an escape game is the genre of the game. The genre is the set of conventions that sets the tone for the entire game. Some of the common genres in escape rooms are escaping an unpleasant place like a dungeon or prison, investigating a mystery or crime, engaging with the supernatural, engaging in intelligence gathering, espionage, or bomb defusal, or planning a heist (Nicholson, 2015). These genres are from recreational escape rooms, so some of the themes are not appropriate for educational escape games, but as a brainstorming activity it can be useful to come up with five different genres to the topic in order to consider what might create the most engaging game.

For example, if the subject for the game was chemistry, then some possible genres and story concepts would be:

- Investigate a crime: the players use chemistry to carry out an analysis of evidence from a crime scene.
- Defuse the explosive device: the players have to analyze the different substances that make up a bomb and use chemistry to create counter-measures for the explosives.
- Escape an unpleasant place: armed with only their chemistry set and their wits, players use different types of chemicals to work through a series of locks and challenges left in their way.
- Help create something: given a challenge (inspired by the real world), the players use their chemistry knowledge to create and test potential solutions.
- Engage with the supernatural: the players use their chemistry knowledge to explore alien/unknown compounds and compare the results to known compounds.

It is critical to select the genre early in the design process, as it will dictate the rest of the decisions made about the game, such as the setting, roles of the players, their adversaries, and the tone of the challenges.

DETERMINING THE PLACE AND TIME

After determining the learning outcomes and the genre, the next step is to decide upon the place and time where the game will be set. The setting of the game determines what types of elements will be most appropriate to develop the challenges from; these elements are known as 'affordances' in game design. An affordance is the quality of an object that communicates a way to use it (Norman, 1988). For example, a game set in a dentist's office could have affordances of an adjustable chair, mirrors, handheld tools, a water jet, a vacuum, patient records, a lightbox for x-rays, toothbrushes, floss, false teeth, or a computer. Challenges that use the types of things that are typically found in a dentist's office will feel more natural and help immerse the players in the game world. Even for a paper-based game, the things that are referred to on the paper should make sense in the setting of the game. Challenges that use things that are not normally found in the environment will make it more difficult for players to immerse themselves in the game. If the game has a genre of 'be an adventurer', then the dentist's office may not the best selection for the narrative.

RED REVEAL

The players find a set of plastic folders for holding A4 paper in different transparent colors. They also find a piece of paper with multi-color writing on it, written and overwritten so much that there is no making sense of it. If the players use the affordances of the folder – that is, it is designed to store paper and is see-through – when they put the paper in the red folder, they will see that it acts as a red-reveal filter, and allows the players to read the secret message.

Similarly, glasses of any color will have players putting them on to look around the room, so you can play the same trick with red-lens sunglasses and a whiteboard.

I often put lab coats and hi-vis jackets in my rooms because players love to use the affordance of wearability, and put them on! Attaching something to the inside of the coat, such as an ID badge, or putting something in an inside pocket can make for a nice surprise for someone who puts the coat on as a lark.

This concept of using affordances that are appropriate extends to the timeframe in which the game is set. Today's dentist's office would feel very different than a dentist's office from 100 years ago or a dentist's office set 100 years in the future. An extension of considering the place and time is also considering the influence of the outside world on the space in which the game takes place. The specific place of a dentist's office may be set in Dubai, London, or a small town in rural Texas; each of these choices may change some of the elements of the room. For example, players in a dentist's office may hear music, talk, and advertisements from that time period on a radio or television in the office. Newspaper stories from the local place and time can provide context for the world outside the office. Supplies and equipment will reflect the region where the office is located, as will other elements that are influenced by culture, such as clothing and personal effects.

The learning outcomes should be kept in mind when deciding upon the setting for the game. If the goal is to teach chemistry, then the setting should be a place where chemistry is important. Escape games, as forms of simulations, are excellent in helping players understand the real-world implications of what they are learning in the classroom. While an alien spaceship in the future might sound like an exciting way to make up content for students to explore, using a man-made spaceship may provide a more meaningful connection for students looking to understand why math and material science matter. This can be useful either as a game before a topic to help players understand why what they will be learning matters in the real world, or afterwards where they can see the application of what they learned.

While being consistent with the time and place is important, using something that is out of place or from a different time can pique interest. Finding a protractor in the dentist's office will draw attention, as it is out of place, but it could indicate that the evil Dr. Log A. Rhythm has been in the space. This should be used strategically to develop the story of the game. If this concept is used too often, it will make it difficult for players to stay engaged with the world, so it should be used sparingly and only when it makes narrative sense.

DEVELOPING THE ROLES OF THE PLAYERS

Another consideration at this point is the roles of the players in the narrative. The traditional escape room role is, 'You are trapped in this unpleasant place and have to get out'. While this is straightforward, it does not provide much guidance to the design process and learning outcomes. For educational escape rooms, the introduction of player roles as an extra layer to a game is valuable. Many of our educational experiences are designed to increase empathy or help players understand the real-world implications of classroom learning, and in these cases, introducing a role for a player is a valuable tool. As part of the expectation of using an educational escape game is that the players will be an active part of the learning process, so giving them an active role in the narrative can be an important part of the design. This role could be explicit, such as telling the players that 'you are an archaeologist', or it could be implicit, where the players discover that by using what they have learned in the classroom in these puzzle-based simulations, they really have become mathematicians or scientists.

JIGSAW METHOD

The jigsaw method of collaborative learning relies on students taking on different roles. In the first phase, the students are separated into groups to learn about a specific topic and develop expertise. In a forensic investigation game, the groups might learn about blood-spatter patterns, fingerprint matching, stomach content analysis, and voice analysis. Then once the teaching or research is done and the skills have been practiced in isolation, the class is grouped so that teams are formed with one expert in each team. The second phase is when these multi-skilled groups, in our case a team of escape game players, work together to apply their skills, teaching each other what they have individually learned as they go.

(Continued)

You could provide role-specific tools or props to bring out the role-playing element of the game, and as a visual confirmation of the earned expertise. Students could take on roles in pairs if the numbers aren't quite divisible.

The jigsaw method was designed in 'The Jigsaw Classroom Study' by social psychologist Elliot Aronson (Aronson and Goode, 1980) to break down stereotypes and prejudice in the multicultural classroom. It makes students work with students they wouldn't normally work with and rely on them for expert knowledge. It's proven to be a powerful technique for building rapport and community amongst all kinds of students.

Table 3.1 Jigsaw method example - crime scene investigation

	Blood spatters	Fingerprints	Stomach contents	Voice analysis
Escape Team 1	Student A	Student E	Student I	Student M
Escape Team 2	Student B	Student F	Student J	Student N
Escape Team 3	Student C	Student G	Student K	Student O
Escape Team 4	Student D	Student H	Student L	Student P

CONFLICT

At this point in developing the narrative, it is valuable to consider the heart of any good story – the conflict. The typical model of a story is that someone wants something, but there is an opposing force. This model introduces two main roles in the conflict – the person (or group) who wants something, and the person (or group or environment) who doesn't want them to have that thing. Each of these primary roles in the conflict can have allies. Finally, there may be people who aren't on either side of the conflict, but who are involved in some other way. At this point, using this model as a brainstorming tool will allow the designer to quickly generate high-level story concepts for the game. Keeping the learning outcomes front and center will help focus the brainstorming on conflicts that will enable exploration of content.

For our dentist's office example, Table 3.2 shows some brainstorming using the model of different roles that the players could take in the game.

One additional step in this brainstorming is to consider the situation where the conflict has already happened, and that the player is investigating. This is akin to the 'someone in the middle' role, but the stakes for the players will be different since the main conflict has occurred. That said, this type of narrative is excellent for creating a twist midway where the players who believe the conflict is over then find themselves embroiled in a new conflict where they are now playing a central role.

Table 3.2 Examples of player roles

Person (or group) who wants something	The players are health inspectors and are coming to the office to investigate complaints of hygiene concerns (health science game).
Ally of person who wants something	A competing dentist suspects this dentist is adding something to the nitrous oxide to make it addictive and wants the players to investigate (chemistry game).
Someone in the middle	Players are in the dentist's office when tornado sirens go off, and the players have to figure out how to find a safe place to ride out the storm (personal safety game).
Ally of person who wants to stop someone from having something	Players are hired as IT professionals for a dentist's office under attack by a hacker trying to steal patient information (computer science and security game).
Person (or group or environment) who wants to stop someone from having something	The players are accountants in the dentist's office, and various parties are trying to get money through different fraudulent tactics (economics game).

CONSIDERING THE ALLIES AND OPPONENTS

Once the role for the player has been decided, then the rest of the conflict needs to be fleshed out. Who or what is in opposition to the player, and how will the player learn about this? In many cases, it is the opposition who is responsible for the challenges and puzzles for the players to overcome. This decision of the opposing force shouldn't be taken lightly, as it is what provides the affordances for the design of the challenges. The challenges also offer an opportunity for the players to learn more about the narrative and the opposition. An evil dentist would create very different challenges than a forgetful dentist, and that would be different still from someone working on the staff who is trying to sabotage the dentist.

If the challenges come from the opposition, then how can the players get help with the challenges? This is where an ally comes into play. The ally can provide the players with tools, instructions, and hints to help them overcome the challenges created by the opposition. For many educational escape games, the instructor will be able to play the role of the ally in order to ensure the students have a good learning experience. The ally can also help the player gain empathy for someone in a certain role in society as they learn about the challenges that this person is facing. The role of an ally is not required for the game, but since the goal is to ensure players explore certain learning outcomes through the game, having the ally as part of the game is a valuable tool to guide the players toward success.

SETTING THE STAGE

While none of this world development is necessary to create a series of challenges that leads the players to unlock a box, it allows the designer to create a more immersive simulation that can help players understand how what they have learned can make a difference. It also makes the rest of the design process easier, as constraints help trigger creativity. Having a specific place allows the designer to create a list of things to use in challenges. Setting a timeframe limits that list and adds context and flavor to the game. Deciding upon the role of the player and the opposition creates the opportunity for developing challenges that the player must overcome. Creating the ally for the player allows for a more natural path to providing tools and hints to overcome the challenge. All of these background pieces are valuable for the next part of the design, which is developing the story and player experience.

REFERENCES

Aronson, E. and Goode, E. (1980) 'Training teachers to implement jigsaw learning: A manual for teachers', in S. Sharan, P. Hare, C. Webb, and R. Hertz-Lazarowitz (eds.), *Cooperation in Education* (pp. 47–81). Provo, UT: Brigham Young University Press.

Nicholson, S. (2015) Peeking Behind the Locked Door: A Survey of Escape Room Facilities. White paper available at http://scottnicholson.com/pubs/erfacwhite.pdf.

Norman, D. (1988) *The Design of Everyday Things: Revised and Expanded Edition* (2nd ed.). New York: Basic Books.

4

CREATING AND SHARING THE NARRATIVE

The narrative is the overarching story that the players experience through the game. Once the constraints and affordances of the world have been developed, and the people and forces in the world have been conceptualized, you are then ready to create the story that connects players to the people and places in the world.

This is a step where many games falter. A story is much more than a theme that provides a backdrop for the game; it should be integral to the activities that the players complete in the game. What the players do should move the story forward. Escape games should put the player in the leading role in a story that they feel they are influencing, with an outcome they believe they can affect.

At the heart of most stories are a few basic concepts:

- Someone wants something.
- Someone else doesn't want that person to have that thing.
- A conflict ensues.

The role of 'someone' could be played by a group of people (a team, an organization, or a group of rag-tag-scrappy-but-lovable-heroes) or by a force of nature, such as a storm, time, or the weather. In the traditional escape room story, this story becomes:

- The players want to escape.
- Someone doesn't want the players to escape.
- A conflict ensues.

As escape rooms explored other models for stories, another common model has developed:

- Someone wants the players to do something.
- Someone else doesn't want the players to do that thing.
- Conflict ensues.

The 'do something' is commonly some type of retrieval mission, where the players are sent to collect something of value, either as the 'good guys' or as 'bad guys'. It also might be an investigative mission, where some type of crime has been committed, and the players are trying to figure out who did it (and perhaps also retrieve something).

The reason why this second model is popular is because it does not require the players to have a prior narrative commitment to the activity. If the story is that the players want to retrieve something, it introduces questions such as 'Why do we want it?' and 'What do we already know about this thing?'. By having it be a desire of someone else, those questions don't need to be answered for the player. This model also introduces an ally for the players, which then provides a narrative-based way to provide clues to the players.

Another important aspect to escape games is that they have a time limit. This time limit needs to be worked into the story at this point. If the designer doesn't think about why the players have only X minutes to do the thing, then adding a clock when running the game will feel artificial. By establishing the reason behind the time limit, the designer has another affordance to use when creating the challenges.

When considering the concept of the story, it is useful to consider the learning outcomes to see if there are any outcomes that can be captured in the story. For example, in a history-based game, the story can be used to help the players understand different perspectives of people involved in a conflict.

THREE-ACT STRUCTURE

After the basic concept of the story has been developed, we need to expand that into a storyline that the players can follow. A useful structure for this expansion is the tried-and-true three-act structure. The three-act structure, which some claim goes back to Aristotle, has been developed by writers over centuries (Lanouette, 1999). While traditional, the three-act structure is a good place for a new escape game designer to start adding structure to a narrative.

Act I starts before the game begins. It starts with any environmental elements the players first encounter, such as music while players are introduced to the game. This is where the players learn where they are and the time period of the game. It is also where the players learn about the 'inciting incident', which is the thing that is at the heart of the conflict. If the players are trying to escape, then this incident will be when they are trapped. If the players are hired to help someone, then this incident might have happened in the past, and the players are brought in to help with the incident. At the end of Act I, the players should have an idea of what they are trying to do and who is opposing them from reaching that goal.

Act II is the longest act and is where the conflict takes place. This is where the players learn details about the different elements of the story and may discover some surprises. They make progress toward resolution, but also suffer some setbacks during this time. The players should figure out what they need to accomplish to be successful at their goal and will be working against the opposing force each step of the way.

Sometime near the end of Act II is a good point in the story for a twist. An easy twist to conceptualize is a shift of one of the elements of the world discussed in the previous chapter. Perhaps their ally becomes their enemy, or they find themselves in a different location. New details may come to the surface that explain prior inconsistencies. By changing something from the original narrative as presented, the twist will re-engage the players for the final act.

Act III is the final steps of the conflict and where the players either succeed or fail. The players should be aware that they are taking on their final challenge and this should require them all to work together. This is a point where many escape-room narratives fail: the players are not aware that they are working on the final task, and the game ends abruptly, or the final task is something that only a few players can do, which leaves the rest of the team standing around while the narrative reaches its conclusion. To have a satisfying ending, the players should know they are working on the final challenge and that final challenge should be something requiring the team to work together.

The narrative should not stop at the end of the final challenge. When the players resolve the final gate, there should be something left to share to help them wind down the narrative. This could be some text that they read, a newspaper article about what happened, or some final engagement with their ally. Too many escape rooms end with, 'Yay! You got out. Take a picture and like us on social media', and don't provide the players with a satisfying conclusion to the story. For an educational game, a post-challenge reflective activity where the players consider the impact of what they have accomplished can serve to help cement the learning outcomes they explored during the challenges.

STORY BEATS

In order to operationalize the narrative, the next step is for the designer to create a series of story beats. Each story beat is where something significant happens in the narrative. There should be story beats that align with each of the desired learning outcomes. If there is a learning outcome without related story beats, then the connection of the game to the learning will feel artificial to the players, as the learning outcome will not be connected to the game.

The story beats are then used as a guide for creating challenges for the game. While story beats can be presented through exposition, that is the least effective way to get the players engaged in the story. It is better to 'show, don't tell', so using elements of the environment to convey the story beat (such as using lighting, sound, video, or physical elements) is better than just exposition, although it may be needed to provide exposition along with environmental storytelling to draw the players' attention to certain elements.

Even better is 'do, don't show' – having the players do things that bring about the story beats is more engaging than using the environment or exposition. To do this, use the story beats as the inspiration for the challenges. Have the challenge be the way that the story beat is conveyed, either through the structure of the challenge, through the activities that the players do for the challenge, or through the resolution of the challenge. It could be that multiple challenges lead up to the resolution of one story beat; in this case, the players need to understand that they are making progress to avoid frustration.

If there are challenges that are not associated with story beats, they will be seen by some players as busywork. Given the limited amount of time we have for our educational escape games, each challenge should have a role to play in reaching the learning outcomes, conveying the narrative, or, ideally, both. This is something new escape-room designers regularly do – they include red-herring puzzles or time-wasting activities to 'keep the players busy' instead of ensuring that each element of the game is there for a narrative-based reason.

When developing the different story beats for the game, it is important to always 'Ask Why' (Nicholson, 2016). While in the real world, things happen for no reason, we should avoid putting things in the game that don't fit into our world. Even if the player doesn't understand why something is happening at the time, there should be a reason it is going on, and the player should be let in on the secrets before the game experience is over. Just like a murder mystery that can't be solved using only the information given to the reader is unsatisfying, the player should understand what was going on in the escape game by the end of the game experience.

To repeat the most important concept thus far: every challenge should matter. Our educational escape games are short, and thus each opportunity to engage the players in a challenge should have a role in advancing the learning outcomes, helping the players to understand their role and environment, and advance the story. Don't waste opportunities by creating non-related challenges.

DEFAULT STORIES

One of the challenges in applying the 'Ask Why' model is that it can be difficult to come up with a world and narrative that connects to the learning outcomes. There are a few default stories that can be used in most situations that will allow the designer to create a narrative framework that makes sense for the players:

1. It's a test/exam/initiation.

   While the narrative of 'it's a test' will allow the designer to include any kind of challenge and have it make sense, it is not a very far departure from the reality of an educational escape game. This is the narrative of our classrooms, so this won't represent much of an escape. To make this narrative more interesting, have the setting of the test be a real-world application of the learning outcomes. For example, students in a physics class might find themselves in a test to become an astronaut, or students learning history might be trying out for a job as a political advisor where their understanding of the past will be important in making decisions about the future.

2. The antagonist is mad or murderous (or both), and wants to see the players struggle to prove their worth.

   While dark, this story concept of the madman who has trapped the players and wants to see if they can prove their worth is at the heart of many escape rooms. It explains why there are challenges and why those challenges can be solved given the materials in the space. It can also explain why the players are getting hints, assuming the antagonist wants to play with their prey. This narrative is harder to connect to a learning outcome, but can work in an absurd way, as the antagonist, for whatever reason, wants to make sure the players really know their English literature. The reality is that this is another version of concept 1, where the players are being tested.

3. The players are dreaming/hallucinating.

   The concept that the players are in a dream can allow anything to happen and have it still make sense. If the players know they are dreaming, this can lead to the players being less inspired to complete the game as they know they will wake up. Adding a threat to the dream moves this in line with the previous story concept, where a madman has created a dream-state with consequences. As above, this also could be used to create an absurd, comedic game, where the players are dreaming during class and having challenges related to the learning outcomes, but taken in unusual directions.

4. The players are following in the footsteps of someone.

   The players are tasked to either prevent someone else from doing something, such as setting up a bomb, or to complete work they didn't finish, such as finishing an antidote to a zombie infection. This set up is useful to introduce a new topic or to give an overview of a series of lessons. The players could have Marie Curie's lab notebook, Thomas Edison's test results, Watson's crime files and evidence folders, or the diary and plans of the evil Dr. Log A. Rhythm to guide them in what they need to do next. The teacher can take on the role of the lab assistant, or the hostage, or whatever character fits the scenario in order to provide hints. Some commercial escape rooms take this approach, and the guide is then optional for experienced players, but a great help for newcomers to escaping.

5. We are being framed/set-up/tricked, and we are told it is one thing, but it is actually one of the above concepts.

   This type of story is focusing on the Act II twist, where the players are told that they are to accomplish one thing, but the reality is that it is a test, a madman, a dream, or someone else's adventure. This can allow for the introduction of different types of challenges and learning outcomes, as the first part of the game can have a different tone and story beats than the second part of the game. If this is used frequently with the same class, players will then be less willing to immerse themselves at the start of a game, as they will be expecting that their initial activities won't have an impact on their success at the overall narrative.

SHARING THE NARRATIVE WITH THE PLAYERS

After developing the world and narrative, the next decision is about how to share this information and what information to share with the players. It is a temptation to try to share everything with the players in a pre-game exposition, but this is a bad idea. The primary reason you have spent this time creating your concepts is so that you can provide a consistent game experience to the players.

When it comes to delivering information about the world and narrative, only a small amount should be presented at a time. Pushing out too much to the players at once will quickly muddle their minds, as you are asking them to take in something in a few minutes that took you much longer to develop. Instead, your goal should be to only give the players what they need at any time, but provide an ongoing drip of world and narrative throughout the experience. Just as the philosophy of 'a little bit often' is a key to success in teaching, it is also key to success in delivering a world and narrative. Take care when presenting 'nice to know' information through the same channels as 'need to know' information to avoid confusing and overwhelming players.

There are different ways to communicate narrative content to students. Given that there is usually a teacher/facilitator leading the activity, one common method is an in-person presentation. This is not very effective if the teacher is reading descriptive text or from a script; students will quickly tune this out in order to 'get to the game', therefore, it is important if it is text to be read out loud that the text be kept short. This is much more effective when the teacher is taking on a role of a character in the world, and will continue to stay in that role throughout the game to help the students work through challenges.

Another common method is through the 'wall of text' delivery, where the students are given a lengthy write-up that talks them through the narrative and the world. Many times, this is quickly read out loud by one student, which has the same impact as having the teacher read a prepared text. Just as before, the wall of text needs to be kept to a few bricks; delivering just what is needed when it is needed is much better than presenting something long up front.

Just as having the teacher act in character can make it easier to engage with up-front content, giving the students roles and scripts can make it easier for them to engage. By dividing up the players, giving each a character and a few lines, it ensures that more participants will engage more closely with at least some of the content. It can also help the players build empathy for the characters in the game, as they will have a better understanding of that character's perspective on the world. This is what we do in the sample game to help players understand both sides of the ethical issue.

Using visual content can help overcome some of the challenges of a long textual presentation. Even having a single picture to set the environment can quickly help players understand the world in which the game is set. Creating a slide deck of images to use as a pre-mission briefing will make a longer presentation more palatable than just the words without images. Introducing theme music and sound effects can quickly teleport the players to a different place, which they could never reach through words alone. Simple comic-book style pages that combine images and words can be a useful tool to make something the students can examine at their table that tells more of a story than plain text.

Another route is to create a pre-recorded video. This has become a common method of presenting information to players in escape rooms. If it is a video of someone reading a script, then it will have the same impact as someone reading the script in person. But if it uses costumes, images, sounds, and scenery, then a pre-recorded video can help the students to understand their world and narrative.

An important concept that we will refer to throughout this book is *environmental storytelling*. As it sounds, this is the concept of conveying a story through the environment. This starts with the setting for the game and continues into delivering the narrative. Disney is a master at environmental storytelling, as their attractions are developed with a narrative base, but most of the concepts are conveyed implicitly through the setting instead of explicitly through exposition.

CONVEYING THE NARRATIVE THROUGH CHALLENGES

The best way to help your players engage with your world and narrative is through your puzzles and other challenges. While the methods listed above can work, they are all external to the core player loop of an escape game – overcoming challenges.

By integrating the narrative and world into challenges, it greatly increases the immersion of the players into that world. This can be done by creating the challenges out of things that would be found in that world and setting, requiring activities that help students take on the role of who they are supposed to be in that world, and using the challenges to convey the story beats. Don't make challenges be superficial obstacles players that have to cross to then be rewarded by more story; make the challenges themselves convey the story.

SETTING THE STAGE FOR THE CHALLENGES

By putting the steps in Chapter 2 and Chapter 3 together, you should have a process to follow to get started with your game.

- Start with the learning outcomes. These should always be at the forefront of your mind, and at each step of this process, ask if there is a way to connect what you are creating to the learning outcomes.
- Decide upon the genre for the game. The genre sets the groundwork for the emotions, the world, the people in that world, and the story. The genre can change during the twist in the story, but having a genre in mind helps the rest of the decisions have some consistency.
- Determine where and when the game is set. Considering the learning outcomes, decide upon where the game is set, both for the setting of the game (where the players are doing their challenges) and at the macro level (what part of the universe the game is set), and in what time period the game is set.
- Populate the world. Document who has occupied the space where the game is set, and what implications that has upon the affordances for challenges in that space. Decide who will be in opposition to people who have occupied that space and consider how these people might interact with the players.
- Decide upon the core story. Using the people in the world and the players, develop the core concepts of who is trying to get something, what they are trying to get, and who or what is trying to stop that from happening. Decide upon the role of the players in relation to the people in the world.
- Develop the three acts. Flesh out the core story using the three-act structure of an introduction, the development of the conflict, a twist, and the resolution of the conflict.
- Create story beats. List out each of the key moments in the story that the players will experience, in the order that they will encounter them.

Now that you have completed this process to develop the narrative, you are ready to create your challenges.

REFERENCES

Lanouette, T. (1999) A History of Three-Act Structure. Available online at www.screentakes.com/an-evolutionary-study-of-the-three-act-structure-model-in-drama/.

Nicholson, S. (2016) Ask Why: Creating a Better Player Experience Through Environmental Storytelling and Consistency in Escape Room Design. Paper presented at Meaningful Play 2016, Lansing, MI. Available online at http://scottnicholson.com/pubs/askwhy.pdf.

5 CONCEPTS FOR PUZZLE DESIGN

WHAT IS A PUZZLE?

There are a variety of definitions of puzzles, but here we are going to focus on a definition that will be useful to you in designing your escape games. It is a simple definition – *a puzzle is a game with a known outcome*. Puzzles, at least for the design of escape games in this book, have a fixed starting state, and the puzzle designer creates the start and the goal to create an interesting journey for the players. Fulfilling one or more tasks becomes the tool by which the player shows that they understood the trick of the puzzle, and in an educational escape game is how they reach the learning outcomes.

CREATING A PUZZLE

When you create a puzzle, there is a process to be followed to ensure all key elements of the puzzle are created. For a puzzle in an educational setting, the first part is to consider the learning outcome that the puzzle is going to support. Every puzzle in an educational escape game is an opportunity to develop a learning outcome, and designers should avoid putting in puzzles 'just for fun' that don't support a learning outcome. Throughout this process, you will learn about different places where content can be integrated into the puzzle to support learning outcomes. Therefore, the first step is to determine which learning outcomes this puzzle will support, to understand what the players know before they start the puzzle, and what they should know after completing the puzzle.

Puzzles are also the opportunities to engage the players with the story beats in an interactive way. The second step is to determine which story beat the puzzle is aligned with, what the players perceive about the story before the puzzle, and what the players should understand about the story after the puzzle.

LINEAR VS. NON-LINEAR GAMES

When creating an educational escape game, it is usually better to create a linear game, where everyone on the team is working on each challenge together. If you have developed each puzzle to advance the learning outcome and the story, then if some of the team does not work on a specific puzzle they will miss out on those key elements.

In a non-linear game, the players may encounter the elements of the game in a different order than was designed, so it is important to ensure that each of the puzzles in a non-linear game is self-contained and do not depend upon the players completing challenges in a certain order to understand the learning outcomes and the story. If the escape game is designed so that the team can split up and different people can work on different puzzles at the same time, it is important that each group still explore the same learning outcomes. A metapuzzle can serve as the reflective activity to bring everything together for the learners.

Escape games are immersive games and, as such, should have puzzles that make sense in the fictional world that has been created for the game. In Chapter 2, we explored how to create that world, and now is the time to return to those thoughts before developing the puzzle. This is the time to 'Ask Why' (Nicholson, 2016): Why is this challenge in the fictional world? Who created the challenge? Who else has tried to solve the challenge, and what roles are the players in such that they are the ones to conquer the challenge?

After determining the learning outcomes, the setting, and the reason why the puzzle exists, then you are ready to create the puzzle. There are a number of elements of the puzzle that are now developed at the same time. This will be an iterative process, where you will start with one of these elements, then develop another element, then return to the first one and tweak it, and continue until you have created your 'game with a solved state' that is the puzzle. The puzzle will consist of components that are manipulated according to rules within a set of boundaries with the help of feedback in order to achieve a goal.

In order to help you understand each of these elements, here is a quick example using a crossword puzzle. The components in the crossword puzzle are the letters. The boundaries in the crossword puzzle are the interconnected boxes. The feedback is that the words cross over and share letters. The rules in the crossword puzzle are the clues and the overarching rule that the letters have to form words that match with the numbered clue. The goal is to fill in all of the boxes with letters that answer the clues. Therefore, as the player explores the puzzle, they manipulate the components (letters) within the boundaries (boxes), following the rules (clues), and checking their work through feedback (intersections) to achieve the goal (fill in all the boxes). Note that we don't recommend the use of a crossword puzzle in your escape games, as they rarely make narrative sense and are a series of factual questions that don't apply to a real-world application of a learning outcome.

COMPONENTS

The components in a puzzle are the elements that the players manipulate. This can be physical manipulation like the pieces in a jigsaw puzzle, things that are written down like a word puzzle, or things that are manipulated in the mind like an observational counting puzzle. If there are hidden objects in an escape room, they are frequently components for a puzzle. These objects may be 'hidden in plain sight'; they are all visible at the start of the game, but the players aren't aware that they are important until they find other pieces of information. The components are one way in which the players can be immersed in the game world. Working with something that is historical in nature, such as old records, or something applied to the domain, such as flasks for a chemistry room, helps the players to engage more deeply with the game. This also can provide an opportunity to meet a learning outcome, if the manipulation is in line with how these components are manipulated in the real world.

One tool the designer has to adjust the difficulty of a puzzle is to add extra components, so that not everything is needed. If the players have the exact components they need, then if they solve almost everything, they can use trial and error with the remaining components to solve the puzzle. This might allow them to skip some steps in the solving process, and if there is a learning outcome tied into the puzzle, can reduce the impact of the game. If there are extra components, then it will be more difficult for the players to use a shortcut to reach a solution. The designer should be careful not to add red herrings and guessing; players should be able to solve the puzzle and know exactly what components are the correct ones.

CREATING PUZZLES FROM REAL-WORLD CONCEPTS

In a game designed to teach accounting concepts, players had a puzzle to determine which of two companies was more profitable. They had the profit and loss statements from two companies and instructions from their ally to direct them.

(continued)

This puzzle had several tasks: the players had to select the relevant information from the profit and loss statement from Company 1, then combine this information to determine the profitability of Company 1. They had to do the same tasks for Company 2, then compare the two profits, and finally answer the question, 'How much more profitable was Company 1 than Company 2 in the last financial year?' by subtracting the calculated profits in order to determine the number for the padlock, and enter that number correctly. The trick of this puzzle was determining what information from the profit and loss was relevant, and knowing how to combine that information to come up with a comparable single number from each statement.

Figure 5.1 Puzzle format for an Accountancy game

More about this puzzle and the game from which it came, 'Death by the Book', can be found in Chapter 7.

BOUNDARIES AND RULES

The boundaries on the puzzle provide the structure for the players to manipulate the components. The boundaries provide an excellent opportunity for both learning outcome and story beat integration. Using historical maps, forms, or grids to fill in from the real world, or physical items that replicate real-world functionality benefit the players and their understanding of real-world content. The boundaries can also be part of the discovery process. A map on a table may not appear important at the beginning of the game, but when the players find placards that stick onto magnets that are embedded under the map, they realize that they have found a puzzle.

The rules are how the components are manipulated within the boundaries to reach the goals. They are the guide to the players as to how to move from the start state to the end state. The players have faith that if they follow the rules provided to them, they will be able to solve the puzzle. To create a fair puzzle, it is important that the rules for solving the puzzles are applied consistently; players can't be expected to break the rules for puzzle solving without some nudge to do so.

These rules might be something that was taught previously to students. For example, if students have already seen the substitution of letters for numbers in their education, then puzzles based on algebra may be presented without rules, and can be useful as a formative assessment tool. This can be quite powerful when the players encounter a real-world application of something they have only learned in theory in the classroom, but find that by applying the rules they have learned, they can solve the challenge.

As you gain experience in creating puzzles, you will want to explore creating your own puzzle structures and rules. There are different ways that the rules can be conveyed to the players. The easiest way is to explicitly provide the rules for the puzzle. Even for a puzzle that many students might know, it can provide a more even playing ground if the rules are explicitly provided. A challenge with providing explicit rules is maintaining immersion within the game world. One route is to not worry about it, and just accept that it can be better for the learning experience to have the learners working on puzzles instead of trying to ascertain what the rules are. If the desire is to use the puzzle to help immerse players in the world or help them understand the other people/forces in the world, the rules can be written as part of the immersion and narrative. For example, if the players have an ally, then the rules could be instructions written in the narrative voice of the ally. If the world is a technological world, then the players could find a manual for the 'device' that contains the puzzle. If the players are hot on the heels of a dastardly villain, then they could find a memo left by the villain for their henchmen with instructions about what needs to be done. In the sample game in Part 3, the 'Spot the Bots' is a puzzle with explicit rules which specify how to determine bot accounts that the players apply to social media profiles and a discussion forum.

Another method of presenting constraints to the players is through implicit rules. This is best done in a puzzle that has physical elements. For example, the traditional number sliding puzzle has the explicit rules of the goal of putting the numbers in order from 1–15, in rows that first go across, and then down. But the structure of the physical slider introduces other rules – that numbers can only be moved if they are adjacent to the single empty space and that they are exchanged with the empty space. A jigsaw puzzle also has implicit rules that are enforced by their physical structure. The advantage to implicit rules is that it can create a playful situation where students can explore the puzzle and learn through exploring the constraints. The disadvantage is that players can get creative in how they manipulate the components and end up ruining the puzzle, making it unsolvable, or solving it without developing the learning outcomes. In the 'Authenticator Access' puzzle in the sample game in Part 3, the players have to figure out how to determine what numbers make up the PIN number, and the method used is different for some of the digits.

A third method of working with the rules for the puzzle is by not presenting them explicitly, but requiring the players to figure out the rules as they work with the puzzle. In these puzzles, part of the puzzle is figuring out the rules of how the components are manipulated to get from the start state to the finish state. This is ideal when the process of figuring out the rules falls in line with the learning outcomes or is designed to help the players gain a better understanding of the world or characters in the game. It is important that these puzzles provide significant feedback to help players from being frustrated with an all-or-nothing solution to the puzzle. Another tool useful to help the players avoid frustration are exemplars, which the players can use to ascertain what the rules might be. In the 'Correct' metapuzzle in the sample game in Part 3, players have to realize that they need to fill in the spaces that correspond to the codes they have gotten from other puzzles, realize that this spells a word, and have the 'a-ha' moment that the word 'Correct' is what they needed to find.

For example, a puzzle designed to teach safety in using lab equipment may require the players to determine the order in which to connect and activate different components. Rather than provide the players with explicit instructions, the puzzle could be built around understanding the different fail states, learning why things are unsafe, and how to correct their procedures to discover the correct solutions.

FEEDBACK

An essential element to include in the design of a puzzle is feedback. Feedback allows the players to build confidence in their actions and to build on prior successes. The most common form of feedback is when the players have manipulated the elements of the puzzle to reach the goal. This goal might be to completely fill out the paper puzzle, to open the padlock, or to fulfill all of the conditions of the puzzle. The moment of finishing the maze or popping the padlock always brings excitement, as the players know they have accomplished something. When an element in the challenge provides the feedback, such as a padlock, the players have a sense that they made an impact on the world.

More subtle, but important, are other forms of partial feedback that occur during the solving process. Partial feedback helps build confidence in the players by letting them know that they are on the right track to solving the puzzle. A good example of partial feedback comes from crossword puzzles; when the player solves two words that share a letter, which provides partial feedback that their answers may be correct.

More importantly, if the player solves two words that are supposed to share a letter but do not share the same letter, the players knows for sure that at least one of the words is incorrect. When solving an algebra problem, players may discover that their substitutions of numbers for letters results in one of the equations being correct, then they have partial feedback.

It is useful to think of feedback provided during the puzzle in one of three ways:

- Definite yes: telling the players that what they did was correct.
- Definite no: telling the players that what they did was incorrect.
- Maybe: telling the players that what they did may be correct and they should continue.

One way to develop 'definite yes' feedback that encourages players to continue is to create a multi-stage puzzle, and when the players successfully complete a stage, they know they have mastered the concepts of the puzzle. This creates an opportunity to make the puzzle more difficult or add a twist to the puzzle to keep the rest of the puzzle from being a mundane task. For example, a maze of electrical circuits might be presented with several stations that have to be visited. When the player reaches one station, they know that they have completed some of the maze and that they can continue from there. In the 'Fake News' challenge in the sample game in Part 3, the use of three articles allows feedback in a way that using two articles did not, in that each of the fake articles has something different to the one true article. If there were only two articles, there would be no confirmation as to which was true and which was false.

A design tool for providing partial feedback to the players is to have aspects of the puzzle that interact or are dependent upon each other. The answer to one part of the puzzle could be the start point for the next part of the puzzle, or the answers from several parts of the puzzle could be combined into a single answer. For example, if the players are instructed to take the first letter from each answer to a series of questions to create a word or phrase, then this provides ongoing 'definite no' feedback if the letters don't make sense, maybe feedback throughout, and 'definite yes' feedback if there is some other type of clue to the final answer that confirms their word or phrase is correct. An example of this is the 'Spot the Bots' challenge from the sample game in Part 3, where the goal is to determine what the bots have in common. If the players get anything other than a location, there isn't a logical next step for that information. Providing a map to the players gives confirmation that the location information is of value.

One thing to be careful of when designing feedback is to avoid providing false feedback. For example, a maze could be created where the player works their way very near the end, but that ends up being a dead end that doubles back to the start. A puzzle that results in a word where the players are to come up with an anagram can be frustrating if there are multiple anagrams for the words that all fit in the lock or make sense with the clue. Once a player has correctly solved a puzzle, they should be confident that their answer is correct when they submit it for validation. One method to resolve false positives is to provide the players with a partial solution, such as one of the letters in the answer word, in order to eliminate alternatives that might be correct. It is difficult for the designer to catch false feedback without playtesting, as the designer will focus on the correct way to solve the puzzle. Playtesters will discover other paths to reach credible answers that the designer did not intend.

Another type of false feedback to be aware of is a false negative. This is common with padlocks, where players have the correct answer but make a mistake in entering the answer, so get negative feedback when they should be getting positive feedback. Directional and combination locks are the most susceptible to this problem, as these locks do not let players see what they have attempted to enter in the way that a multi-dial number or letter lock allows. This can be a challenge to catch, as the students can get frustrated when they try the lock and it doesn't work.

GOAL

The goal is the solved state for the puzzle. The goal creates one more opportunity to provide support to the narrative, if the goal matches a goal of one of the characters in the story. It also creates an opportunity to add support to a learning outcome if the goal represents something that maps to a concept related to what the students are learning.

After determining the goal, the designer also needs to decide how the players learn about the goal. One option is the *specific goal*, where the players know what the solved state is and need to reach that goal. A good recreational example of this are the classic tangram puzzles, where the players see the shape that all of the pieces must be used to create, but do not know how those pieces combine to create that shape (see Figure 5.2).

The specific goal can also be used to create a communication challenge, where some players see the goal and must communicate to other players what the goal looks like. An example of this in the sample game in Part 3 is the 'Final Decision', where the players are presented with two choices and must pick one of them; the importance of this challenge is the debate and process to decide, as the 'solution' of picking a choice is a trivial act of selecting and opening a sheet of paper.

Another option is an *unspecific goal*, where the players are provided with constraints or parameters that they need to meet. The most common unspecific goal in puzzle boxes is the three- or four-digit lock, where the players know they need to use the puzzle to generate a three- or four-digit number, but don't know what that number is. Another common puzzle type that uses unspecific goals are logic problems where the players are given a set of constraints and have to find the one combination of answers that meets those constraints. One challenge when creating a puzzle with an unspecific goal is to ensure that there are not multiple answers that meet the constraints. For example, if the goal is to get a four-digit padlock open, you need to take

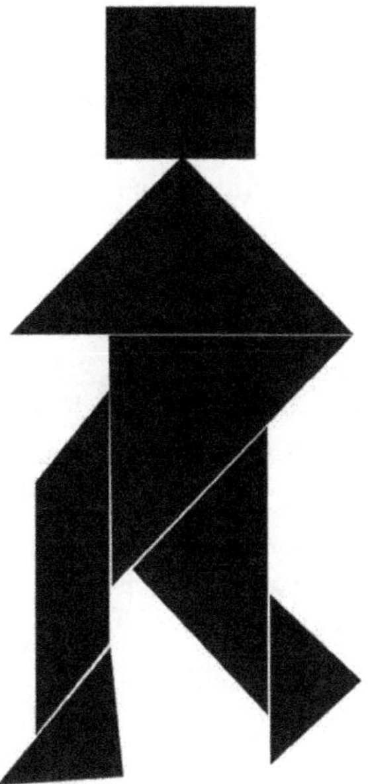

Figure 5.2 Tangram puzzle (solved)

care that there are not multiple four-digit numbers that can be generated by the puzzle and that any extraneous four-digit numbers (such as a year) are removed. If this is not possible, then you can add an additional constraint to help the players know which of the four-digit numbers are the correct one. In addition, if there are multiple four-digit padlocks in the game, they should be marked in a way so that players know which padlock is the correct one for a puzzle. In the sample game in Part 3, the 'Authenticator Access' puzzle is unspecific, as the players know that they need to find a four-digit PIN, and the puzzle is figuring out four digits and the correct sequence.

A third option is an *unknown goal*, where the players are given components and must manipulate them in order to reach the goal of the puzzle, but it is not clear up front what that goal is. This is commonly known as an 'a-ha' puzzle, as it requires the players to take a leap from what they have to what they need to do with it. For example, providing text to the players using a stretched font requires the players to have the 'a-ha' that they need to pick up the paper, rotate it, and look across the top of it in order to read the font (see Figure 5.3).

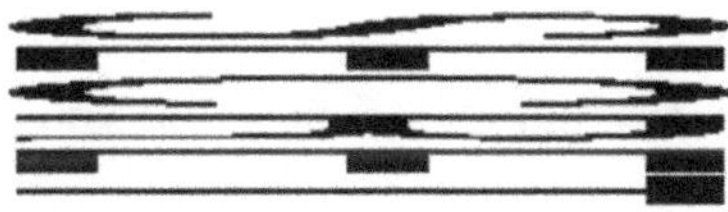

Figure 5.3 Stretched word puzzle

Giving the players a strip of paper with letters on it and a round dowel requires the players to have the 'a-ha' to wrap the paper diagonally around the dowel to reach the message down the side. The unknown goal puzzle may also be just the first stage of a longer puzzle, where they solve the 'a-ha' to learn what their goal is, and then use a process with the components to reach the goal. In the sample game in Part 3, the 'Spot the Bots' final challenge of 'find something in common' is an unknown goal, as it is nebulous; the players first have to look at possible elements that all three bots share, then look at other information provided (the maps), and then see what the locations all have in common.

The challenge with an unknown goal puzzle is that it is not as easy to determine how long it will take players to have the epiphany that leads to the 'a-ha', so feedback is important. One method of feedback is through signposting, where the puzzle creator builds in small nudges that help confirm the ideas that a player has. For example, in the paper-wrapping puzzle mentioned above, if the paper has been pre-wrapped around the dowel so it has a slight curve, that will hint to the player what is to be done. If the ends of the paper are cut on an angle and the letters are printed on the same angle, so that they are read in a straight line once wrapped, it will provide feedback to the players that they are on the right track. Providing the user map in the 'Spot the Bots' challenge in the sample game is the signposting to help the players solve the puzzle. Good feedback in the puzzle design should provide a similar role to the teacher watching the students work and providing verbal confirmation that what they are doing is correct. Conversely, it is important to ensure that elements of the puzzle that might lead players down the wrong path are removed; it can be difficult to identify these elements until the puzzle is playtested.

CONSIDERING LOCKS AND ADDING LAYERS

At this point in the puzzle design, it is important to consider how the players will know if their answer is correct. A common method for this in escape games is to have the players input the answer into some kind of padlock. Table 5.1 lists many of the common padlocks, what affordances they allow, and any notes about using them. It is recommended to purchase locks where you can set the combination instead of having to create puzzles that lead to the one specific pre-set combination – they are marketed as 'resettable'. You may also like to consider that some makes of combination locks have a version with a master key, which makes it so much faster to reset the lock if you use the same padlocks for multiple games, and you'll never lose a padlock to a forgotten or mis-dialed code.

Table 5.1 Common locks

Type of padlock	What it allows	Notes
Key	A specific physical key	Finding a key doesn't lead to many learning outcomes, and is easy to lose.
Three-digit	0–9, 0–9, 0–9	Easy to open without the code by trying each possible combination. Briefcases typically have two independent three-digit locks.
Four-digit	0–9, 0–9, 0–9, 0–9	Most common lock. Using too many of them will confuse players as to what answer goes in which lock. Some have colored dials, which can be useful.
Five-digit	0–9, 0–9, 0–9, 0–9, 0–9	Some have colored dials – you can use the colors to clue the order of the digits.
Combination lock/safe dial	Typically 0–40, 0–40, 0–40, alternating direction	Not recommended, as players don't know if their answer is wrong or if they entered it incorrectly. It is difficult to use and to write puzzles for.
Four-dial or five-dial letter lock (fixed)	A subset of letters on each dial creating many common words	If the manufacturer publishes the wordlist, you know every lock is identical – vital for large-scale team games.
5-dial letter/ Number lock (interchangeable rings)	5 rings, each with a set of numbers or letters, use in any order	With only one lock, you have to use a combination of numbers and letters; to use all numbers or all letters, you need to purchase two locks. Replacement/unusual rings can also be 3D printed.
Push-button	A subset of digits, none of which repeat	Order does not matter in many styles of these locks, which can be useful in puzzle design.
Date	DD-MMM-YY	Tempts the players to try every date in the room, including today's date, but still useful.
Directional	A series of up, down, left, right directions	Can be frustrating for players, as players don't know if their answer is wrong or if they entered it incorrectly. Avoid long sequences. Very flexible, as any value can be assigned to each direction.
Emoji	A variety of emojis	For specific themes and puzzles – a game about social media for example, or empathy – these could be perfect.

DIRECTIONAL LOCKS

Directional locks come with stickers that allow you to change each of the four points into representations of a cipher. So instead of up, down, left, right, or north, east, south, west, you can replace these with the suits in a pack of cards or colored dots. You could also use numbers or letters in each of the directions, and you aren't restricted to just four, as each direction can represent more than one variable. They could be the planets or the notes on a musical scale. They can have more than four directions in their answer, but the longer the answer, the more likely the players are to make a simple mistake. You don't need to have all of the options stuck onto the padlock - you can simply provide a diagram to act as a key for the code. For example, in a historical game, you may ask players to work through correspondence between explorers and governments, and then fill in the blanks:

___________ was commissioned by the ________ government to explore ___________ in ______.

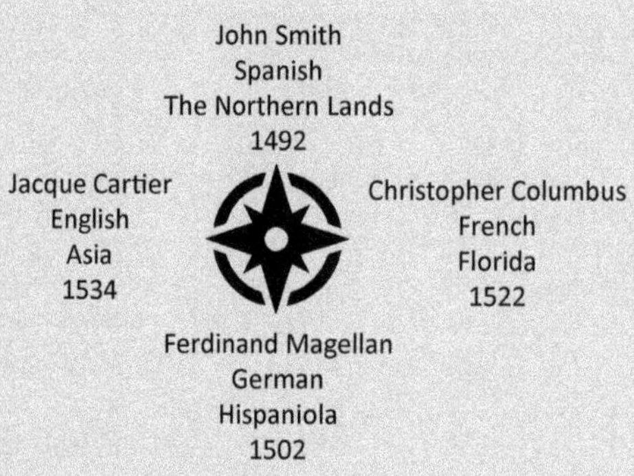

John Smith
Spanish
The Northern Lands
1492

Jacque Cartier
English
Asia
1534

Christopher Columbus
French
Florida
1522

Ferdinand Magellan
German
Hispaniola
1502

Figure 5.4 Directional lock guide

With a directional lock and this guide, the players can do research using the correspondence to discover the answer.

In many recreational escape rooms, designers are moving away from physical locks and toward using digital solutions such as magnets to hold containers closed, and radio frequency identification (RFID) tags embedded in objects to create more 'magical' experiences. Another solution, as discussed earlier, is to use Google Forms to create a digital version of locks, although there is a charm to unlocking something physical in the real world after figuring out a challenge.

There are several other ways of adding a game element that functions like a physical lock, but do not require the resources for physical locks. The first is a social lock, where the players write down their answer and bring it to the facilitator, and then receive the next container from the facilitator. This could be written into the storyline as a password to be given to the 'agent' to continue. While this will work well to gate content, it does run the risk of creating a bottleneck in the game as players queue up to give their passwords to the agent. The 'Envelope Game', discussed in Chapter 2, presents a model where each team also serves as agents for another team, and each team's puzzles resolve to different answers.

Another method is the 'honesty lock', which asks the player to fulfill a condition to move on in the game. This might be an envelope that says 'Do not open until instructed' or 'Only open if the combination of digits in your answer is 27'. It can also be more complicated, as in the sample game, where the players fill in shapes based upon their answer to create the word 'Correct'. You could also use a look-up table, such as the fingerprint table in the sample game, where players look up their answers to several puzzles to get instructions on how to continue. This could also be done with numbered paragraphs, where players visit a specific paragraph based upon their answer, and this 'book of codes' is used throughout the entire game. Many of the at-home escape games use some type of honesty lock, such as a code wheel that you dial your guess into, to allow the players to facilitate their own game.

Adding Layers

Sometimes a puzzle is straightforward, a simple problem is presented, and the code that results is a four-digit number that is input into a lock exactly as it is found; all the digits in the same order. However, there is an opportunity for educators to add a second layer to the puzzle, requiring the players to determine the order of the digits in the lock. This means that one layer can be more of a puzzle and the other layer is the task, or the demonstration of learning, although both parts can lead to learning objectives.

You can put more than two layers into a puzzle to make it more interesting, or more collaborative, or to demonstrate higher-order skills (HOTS) by making it harder, and requiring the application of a number of skills to solve. The layers can also be used to convert the solution of the puzzle into something that will go into a lock. This is also how learning objectives are organized, building from the lower-order thinking skills (LOTS) to the HOTS. Breaking down a puzzle into layers can be a great aid to game design, and to the playtesting process. Adding layers generally makes a puzzle more difficult while removing them makes it easier. Testing each layer separately is also a way of determining which, if any, layers of the puzzle are the most problematic for players, and if this is not intentional, allows you to simply swap out or edit the part causing the problem, rather than scrapping the whole puzzle.

As game designers, we need to disguise the task within the puzzle, like hiding the cabbage in the mashed potato. If the students are to demonstrate that they can solve quadratic equations, they could be given four equations to solve. If the equations were numbered one to four, this would also give the order of the answers to be given, and hence the order of the code. This would simply be a new format for an old question with an additional constraint that all the answers are within the range 0–9 (to match the padlock), but it wouldn't be a puzzle. It would be a worksheet with a lock to validate the answers (see Figure 5.5).

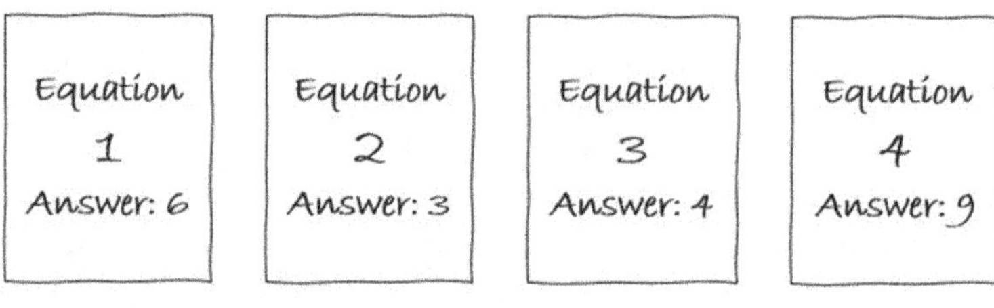

Figure 5.5 Direct conversion of answers to code

So how to add layers to make this into a puzzle? Well, the learning objective is to solve the quadratic equations, so we can't remove the need for the players to discover the values, but we can think of different ways of them establishing the order of the digits. If the first equation is in a circle, the second in a triangle, the third in a square, and the fourth in a hexagon, then the answer is ordered by the number of sides to each shape (see Figure 5.6). If each equation is in a different color and a padlock has colored tumblers, then the players need to have the 'a-ha!' realization to match the colors of the equations to the tumblers. It would be even better if there was a narrative reason why the equations exist, and this reason then leads players to figure out the order of the answer, so that the puzzle provides both a learning outcome and a story beat.

If you want to add a layer to a puzzle like this, there's a tool to help. In his book *Information Anxiety*, Richard Wurman (1990) identifies five ways of organizing information: location, alphabet, time, category, and hierarchy (LATCH). LATCH is useful for when you want to add a layer to a puzzle based on organizing information.

Location is where things belong in relation to each other if you were mapping something out, so as well as the obvious map or a globe, this could be a diagram of the human body, blueprints of an airplane, the planets in the solar system, the stars in the night sky, or the colors of the rainbow. This is an opportunity to connect the players to another learning outcome or to use environmental storytelling to connect into the narrative.

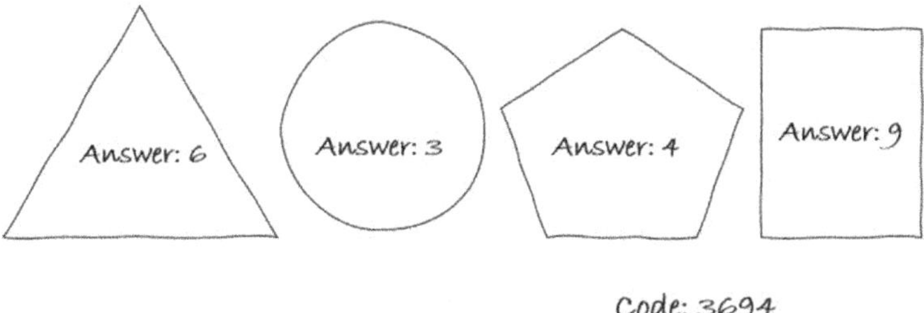

Figure 5.6 Layered conversion of answers to code

Alphabet is useful for large bodies of information that have to be sorted through and then have records eliminated or aggregated in some way. Some students may not yet understand the higher-order concepts of hierarchies or categories, so having to sort and perhaps resort by alphabet on different records would not be trivial for them. This may also be useful when working with a different language, as having to re-order items using the letter order from another language can provide a learning outcome and/or environmental storytelling.

Time is an easily understood framework, although understanding its representation can be tricky for some. Some players might not know the 24-hour clock, and some might not know how to read an analogue clock face. Similarly, with representations of dates, these need to be consistent across the room in every instance if you don't want to mislead the team. If you want to use Roman numerals to represent digits in a solution, then you will need to have a key to explain it for at least some of the players. One way to do this is to have a clock with Roman numerals in the same room as a clock with Arabic numerals – or even invent your own code for the numbers, with the clock faces acting as a Rosetta Stone.

Categories work well when you want to organize items of similar importance – color-coding can reinforce this. Getting the players to decide which category something goes in can get them applying their knowledge and debating amongst themselves. It can also help them build empathy by learning how someone in their role would see the world.

Hierarchy is the mode of organization used when you want to signify the relative magnitude or importance of the items. It can apply to physical attributes such as size or weight, but also more complex information structures such as tree diagrams. Again, this can be useful for both learning outcome application and environmental storytelling.

There are plenty of puzzles to be made by mapping one schema over another. For example, a map of the world (L) can have time zones (T); books ordered by size (H) or color (H) can be re-ordered by Dewey Decimal number (C) or author (A); a family tree (H) can be used to indicate directions (L). The periodic table (L, H, and C) on its own provides a wealth of different ways of looking at the information presented.

The puzzle can have additional learning outcomes, or simply be made to feel more like a puzzle by adding layers. For example, if the person who left the equations behind was afraid of someone finding them, they might have written the equations in UV pen, and the players need a blacklight to find them. If the equations and the other variables needed to solve them are on different safety placards, all out of sight of each other, solving the equation will require group communication skills, delegation, problem solving, and leadership. These additional layers are an opportunity to add depth to the narrative, to introduce characters, props, or further information around the context and content of the learning. The puzzles and the narrative should work entirely in harmony, and by designing a puzzle in layers this becomes much easier.

However, when you have several layers to the puzzle, you could unintentionally build in opportunities for the players to divert themselves. If they get an early layer of the puzzle wrong, they could follow a path to a solution, and only discover they are wrong when they get to trying to open the padlock. As with all learning, the players need formative feedback to help them know they are on the right track. Returning to the equations example above, if at the point of solving the equations the answers are not single whole digits, the players know they have gone wrong and will try again before attempting to open the padlock, even if they have already figured out how to get the order from the shapes. It simply isn't a possible correct solution yet.

In the sample game in Part 3, the 'Authenticator Access' puzzle has several layers. First, the players have to look at the individual pictures to figure out which digits in the PIN code each could represent. Then, the time codes on the picture help the players determine the order of the code. Finally, coloring in the spaces in the *correct* puzzle gives feedback that they might be right (in conjunction with solving the 'Password Prying' puzzle).

PLAYTESTING PUZZLES

The final (but never ending) stage in puzzle design is playtesting. The first time the puzzle is put in front of someone should not be when you are presenting your games to the class. One reason playtesting is needed is because you have elements of the challenge in your head and forget to document them for the player. You will find that you have made your puzzle too challenging because you did not provide clear and complete directions (or enough signposts for an 'a-ha' puzzle), as you watch playtesters struggle to get started on the puzzle. The other thing that playtesting does is bring to life alternative solutions to puzzles that you never thought of when designing the challenge. A well-designed puzzle has only one solution, so identifying alternative solutions allows you to include additional constraints to eliminate them and avoid player frustration. This is a case where more playtesting is better, as each playtest brings a different set of minds to explore your challenges and find the gaps in what you have created.

Most of the time, you will find that your puzzles are too difficult during the first playtest. Things that are obvious to you as the designer of the puzzle are not obvious to the player, as they are being faced with an array of possibilities, and are trying to decide how to manipulate the components to reach the goal. This is a reason for having signposting and feedback early in the puzzle, so that the players have confidence that they are on the right track. There are several techniques that can be used to make puzzles easier:

- Provide explicit directions. If players do not know how to get started, then providing more explicit directions will help them take those first few steps.
- Provide an exemplar. If it is not appropriate to provide directions, then providing an example puzzle and answer can help, as the player can then examine this in order to determine how the exemplar answer was reached so that they know how to start on their puzzle.
- Create multiple stages. Rather than one large complex puzzle, having several smaller puzzles, each building on the last, can help players to better understand what to do and build their confidence, so that when they reach the final complex puzzle, they have confidence in getting started.
- Remove misleading information and puzzle paths. Red herrings (or clues/puzzles that do not lead to the final goal) are seen by many designers in the escape room industry as a way to 'fill out' a room. The problem with red herrings is that they are frustrating to the player who spent time trying to solve them. In a learning environment, red herrings should only be used when their existence ties into a learning outcome and the players are trying to learn how to identify false information and false leads as part of the activity.
- Develop hints. It is always better to use signposting and feedback within the puzzle instead of hints, as these hints are from an outside source and don't fit in with the rest of the challenge as nicely. But, if it is not possible to create signposting, then having hints that are delivered at set times can ensure that the players stay on schedule to complete the game in the time allowed. Needing a hint to solve a puzzle can also be demoralizing for a player in a way that using signposts and feedback that is built into the puzzle is not, as the player sees these elements as part of the puzzle.

MAKING PUZZLES HARDER

Sometimes, puzzles are too easy. A puzzle that is too easy is less likely to bring about a learning outcome than a puzzle that requires players to stop, read, think, process, and act. There are times when you want to slow the players down, so that they spend more time interacting with the puzzle and exploring the learning outcome. Here are some techniques that can make puzzles more challenging:

- Remove explicit directions. If the players have to figure out what they need to do as well as follow the process of the puzzle, then it will make the task more challenging. In order for this to be successful, additional information may need to be added to the background or components to make it clear what things go together in the puzzle. The directions can also be incomplete, where the players can get started but then must figure out what to do next.
- Add additional layers. As discussed earlier in the chapter, the designer can add additional layers of complexity to make it more difficult to solve the puzzle completely. These layers may require teamwork, communication, or cross-referencing information from different sources to solve the challenge. This could also require them to solve smaller puzzles that then feed answers into a larger puzzle.
- Add distractors. A puzzle can be made more complex by adding elements that are not needed to solve the puzzle. The designer walks a fine line with distractors; if there are too many of these elements, then the puzzle can become frustrating or tedious as players work through many different combinations to come up with the right one. The proper role of distractors is to make it difficult for the players to solve the puzzle through backsolving, where the player starts with the goal or constraints and works backwards to find the solution. A maze is a good example of a puzzle with distractors – if there were no distractors, then it would just be a path to follow without any choices.

MAKING PUZZLES MORE FRUSTRATING

Some puzzle designers confuse making a puzzle harder with making it more frustrating or tedious. These are *not* good ways to make puzzles more difficult:

- Adding red herrings. In this case, red herrings are puzzles or puzzle paths that do not lead anywhere. As mentioned earlier, there is a fine line between red herrings and distractors. In general, if the player has the information in the puzzle to decide what puzzle paths to explore and what to eliminate, then the extra elements to the puzzle are distractors. But if the player has no way to know which is the correct path without trying every combination, then this can be a frustrating red herring. In the maze example given earlier, adding a layer on top of the maze that provides feedback (such as letters that spell a word) can help make the maze a more enjoyable puzzle.
- Making longer processes. While puzzles can be made to take longer by requiring more process work, this doesn't add to the enjoyment of the puzzle. Decrypting

one sentence by learning a decryption code can be enjoyable, but decrypting a paragraph doesn't add anything more to the overall puzzle experience. If the goal is to get students to perform the same task again and again, an escape game is not the best teaching tool for that.

- Adding too many layers. Rather than add another layer to an already complex puzzle, it is better to create a new puzzle. Every layer added to a puzzle increases the amount of work that has to be re-done if one of the elements of that layer is solved incorrectly. It will lead to a better play experience to create a new separate puzzle instead of stacking another layer onto the puzzle.
- Adding elements to 'teach' that aren't related to the puzzles. Over the years, many poorly designed educational games superficially combined quizzes about topics with game mechanisms with the goal of teaching. Escape games offer a similar temptation – it would be simple to take a worksheet from class and make it a 'puzzle' by having the answers turn into a word that unlocks a lock. But a worksheet isn't a puzzle, and this type of gamification of traditional learning doesn't take advantage of what escape games for learning can offer. Students may find the act of opening a lock to be more engaging than traditional forms of grading, but this type of superficial use of an escape game mechanism will lose its power to motivate over time.

INTEGRATING LEARNING OUTCOMES AND PUZZLE DESIGN

Throughout this chapter, we have explored the different elements of puzzles – the setting, the components, the background, the rules, the goals, and feedback. Each of these elements of a puzzle provides an opportunity for the designer to do one of several things:

- To integrate learning outcomes into the elements of the puzzle.
- To connect the players to the game world and characters within that world.
- To develop the narrative.

Or when possible, all of the above.

CONCLUSION

To close out this chapter, we will develop a puzzle around a learning outcome and demonstrate how different parts of the puzzle can be used in different ways.

Learning outcome: Students will be able to correctly use their, they're, and there.

Setting: The setting is an observational space station outside an alien planet. The players are observing signals from this planet and are providing messages to their allies on the planet as to where the aliens are. If they send the wrong messages or overlap messages, their allies may be in trouble. At this point in the narrative, the players do not know who the aliens are, so refer to them as 'they'.

Rules:

Send messages by drawing lines between the message fragments and the words that correctly fill in the blanks (see Figure 5.7). Be careful not to overlap messages by crossing any lines over each other. Your lines do not have to be straight. Once you have drawn lines to connect messages to their words, count the number of lines leading to 'their', 'they're', and 'there', and enter those digits into the three-digit lock in that order.

Watch out! _________ coming up on _________ right hand side.

Their

_________ eyes are like laser beams!

Over _______ ! _________ spaceship is unguarded, as _______ out on a mission.

They're

_________ looking here, __________, and everywhere for you!

There

Hopefully, _________ big teeth just mean they like to eat really big plants.

Figure 5.7 Their, they're, and there puzzle

DEVELOPING THE NARRATIVE

To develop the narrative for this puzzle, we first thought about the learning outcome. The end goal is to help the students understand that 'their' is used for possessive, 'they're' is used as a shortcut for 'they are', and 'there' is used for a location. We needed to think of a story beat that would have elements of location, possession, and action. We also wanted to use the name 'They' to refer to an aspect of the world; a natural fit would be something that had no name and was typically referred to as 'they', which would be aliens. It also is a narrative and world that has significant depth to explore with other activities in the overarching game.

The next challenge was to think about the goal. Since there will be three different possibilities, and each one will be used a number of different times, then a three-digit lock is a natural fit as the final goal for the players. It doesn't make sense for the learning outcome to have them guess what order to put the numbers in, so that order is presented to the players as a constraint on the goal.

To build out the puzzle, we then took index cards and wrote each of the words and phrases on them, and used string to connect the words to the phrases, moving them around until we had a configuration where no lines were crossing. If we wanted to make the challenge more difficult, we would not present the hint that 'your lines do not have to be straight', and leave that as an unknown constraint for the players to figure out. Having this 'a-ha' requirement doesn't support the learning outcome, so we decided to inform the players up front of that element of the challenge so they can focus on what matters.

Note that the line connection element is a layer on this puzzle. It is not needed to solve the puzzle, as all the players need to do is count the number of times each element is used. But the constraints of the lines not crossing adds partial feedback for the players; if they are crossing lines, then they know something is wrong ('definite no' feedback). If they do manage to draw the lines without crossing, then this is 'maybe' feedback, as it means they are potentially correct. Finally, the activity of drawing the lines is both playful and embraces the narrative concept of sending messages without overlapping them. It adds a little fun to what might otherwise be a drab worksheet.

REFERENCES

Nicholson, S. (2016) Ask Why: Creating a Better Player Experience Through Environmental Storytelling and Consistency in Escape Room Design. Paper presented at Meaningful Play 2016, Lansing, MI. Available online at http://scottnicholson.com/pubs/askwhy.pdf.

Wurman, R. (1990) *Information Anxiety*. New York: Bantam Books.

6 DESIGNING SPECIFIC PUZZLE TYPES

Now that you have a basic understanding of the key elements of any puzzle, it's time to explore specific types of puzzles appropriate for educational escape games. There are common puzzle types that we are not including in this chapter, as they do not lend themselves to learning outcomes. For example, Sudoku is a popular type of puzzle, but there is little connection between Sudoku and learning outcomes. If we talked about how to create Sudoku puzzles, it would encourage you to create one for your games, and that would take away from the learning outcomes and narratives. Therefore, we are focusing on a subset of puzzles that are easily adapted to different learning outcomes. In Chapter 1, we explored our seven-part framework for using escape games in learning, and as this book is focused solely on escape rooms for education, we continue that approach here.

Table 6.1 shows the likeliest matches for puzzle-types against the dimensions of learning in an escape game, but it is not comprehensive. A puzzle may be layered, and in which case a code or cipher layer could add a dimension of difficulty to a puzzle of any other type. We can see how individual puzzle types and even specific puzzle designs meet specific learning objectives, and by layering puzzles using metapuzzles and strong narrative, we can get students to engage in higher order thinking skills (HOTS) such as synthesis and analysis. By starting with the types of learning outcomes you are looking to bring about in the game, you can use Table 6.1 to help you find a starting point in this chapter for a specific puzzle type.

Table 6.1 Most likely matches for learning dimension and puzzle type

Dimension	Puzzle type						
	Factual/ Word	Logic	Deduction	Math	Codes and ciphers	Role playing	Metapuzzles
Setting	⊗				⊗	⊗	⊗
Social	⊗	⊗	⊗	⊗	⊗	⊗	⊗
Story		⊗	⊗		⊗	⊗	⊗
Skills	⊗			⊗	⊗	⊗	⊗
Strategy	⊗	⊗	⊗	⊗			⊗
Simulation				⊗		⊗	
Self			⊗			⊗	⊗

FACTUAL/WORD PUZZLES

When many people think of educational games, they picture games where you are asked a series of factual questions to move ahead on a game board. Because of this, many first-time escape game designers turn to the same model of using trivia-style questions that are answered using padlocks. The resulting game model ends up being something like this: 'You enter the Dungeon of the Dark Master. As you creep down the hallway, a trap springs open at your feet. As you float in midair, you hear a creepy voice that asks: "Who was the first president of the United States to be elected twice?"'

By this point in the book, you hopefully realize the problems with this model. The challenges should immerse the player into your narrative world because they make sense. If factual questions are used in the game, they need to be supported by a world, a story, and characters that make sense. A factual question like this is not a puzzle – it's just a question that you either know the answer to, or don't know the answer to. If you can't figure out a way to make a factual question make sense in the game, then it's better to use a different educational activity to have learners explore the outcome. As escape games take time and resources to create and deliver, they are best used when they will have the most impact.

Another temptation for first-time designers is to rely on more traditional styles of word puzzles. A common example is a word search, where the players circle the words, and then the pattern formed by the circles spells out a four-digit code to put into a lock. Conversely, the letters that are not circled can form the pattern needed for the lock. While this is more of a puzzle than just a question, a word search doesn't address most learning outcomes; matching the patterns of letters to a grid isn't teaching anything about what the words mean.

Crosswords have been used in the past to test knowledge, and for providing a collaborative puzzle that involves the whole team in solving it, but they need some tweaking to work in an escape game. Crosswords are traditionally solitary activities, so using a traditional puzzle creates a situation where one person solves the puzzle while everyone else watches. The puzzle needs to be made larger so that multiple people can work on it, or broken apart so that different sections can be solved at once.

In addition, there are few narrative reasons why a crossword puzzle makes sense in an escape game. Hiding a secret message in the crossword and building around it works well, so that once the crossword is solved, the players can see a password, code, or instructions. There can then be a narrative that supports the appearance of the code-containing puzzle in the scenario, with an ally who is hiding a message to be delivered to the players. The crossword could be used as a metapuzzle, with the players finding the clues as they go along, and slowly building up the crossword grid. In this case, you would have to have an extra reveal at the end, such as a code or secret message. Just finishing the crossword alone would not give enough sense of satisfaction and success.

A similar puzzle could be made from a Scrabble board, with the students perhaps reconstructing a famous grudge match as part of the narrative or that their ally is providing instructions for on how to use the Scrabble tiles as a way to pass along a secret message. Scrabble is useful because each tile also has a number which could be used for transposition to a padlock.

But there are other models for using factual questions as part of a puzzle. The best way to use word or factual puzzles is to think of a real-world situation where the players would need to come up with missing words given clues or constraints. For example, there could be an instruction manual that has been ripped apart, and the players have to use their factual knowledge of the underlying system to reassemble the instructions. There could be an audio message where certain words are covered with static, and the players have to then figure out the missing words to reconstruct the message to give them the directions to continue. A letter that got wet could have words that are blurred. It could be that the setting is a test to ensure that only people with certain types of knowledge can enter a location, and therefore the players must demonstrate their knowledge to continue. By thinking more deeply about real-life situations where words or facts are needed, you can create a more engaging and immersive game.

Words are a rich source of both puzzle and learning material for certain topic areas. Translating words using a French-to-English dictionary is an everyday task, albeit one that you may want the students to learn and practice; if the players were part of a spy support network, they could be responsible for translating messages back and forth between different languages. Translating words across several languages until you come up with the five-letter word that fits the padlock is a puzzle, and with enough dictionaries and languages for every player can allow everyone to participate, although for a puzzle like this, it is useful to provide players with guidance, such as how many letters are in each word.

This language puzzle is a good example of research-based puzzles. In these challenges, the players are given information resources and part of the learning outcomes are to have the players do research on a topic to find the answer to the questions. As always, there should be a narrative reason why the players need to find these answers, but having the challenge be based on doing research for the answers instead of just knowing (or not knowing) the answers provides a more engaging and rich learning activity. A useful model for a research-based puzzle is providing the players with statements where they have to determine what is true and what is false. This is easy to support narratively with an enemy who wants to throw the players off with misinformation, and encouraging students to validate questionable information with reliable resources is always a valuable learning outcome in any field.

OBSERVATIONAL

Observational puzzles require the players to look for something hidden, to seek out patterns, to count related items, or to find something that is out of place. All challenges start with an observational layer. In escape rooms, experienced players first hunt for locks and other gates in the room, and then they hunt for clues, challenges, and components for puzzles that will help them open those gates. For all escape games, the players start by looking over the papers, containers, and other materials to determine what challenges they are facing. With escape games for learning, it is important to consider the role of this type of searching in achieving the learning outcomes; after all, if the players spend ten minutes hunting through a stack of papers, that is ten minutes that weren't spent on activities that would help them move closer to the learning outcomes.

As with all puzzles, start with the learning outcomes and look for those places where observing a pattern would help with a concept. For example, for a mathematics class, looking at problems that are worked out for errors would make sense, especially if the narrative involved an ally who is a mathematician leaving behind the code to a lock 'in plain sight' for the players to find. For a history class, the players may be time travelers looking to find where their time-traveling opposition has gone into the past and changed history. A team of chemistry detectives can review the notes of someone to determine what was wrong that caused the mysterious explosion. In the sample game, the players are comparing three different websites for clues as to which are fake and which are authentic.

There are also times where observational elements are used to convey the narrative and create the gate, although they may not advance the learning outcome. This should only be done if these elements are adding a puzzle-like layer to another challenge that is related to the learning outcomes. For example, in the 'One-Box Wonder' presented in Chapter 2, the players first solve four puzzles that are related to the learning outcome. They then count colored objects that relate to the colors of the individual puzzles to determine the order in which to enter the digits in a combination lock. Many of the layers of LATCH discussed in the previous chapter can be used in this way, where the players take what they have solved and then engage with a second observational layer to transform that information into a phrase or number used to get through a gate.

Observational activities are also at the heart of 'a-ha' puzzles. 'A-ha' puzzles are those where you present the player with several different components and they have to figure out what goes together. If there are learning outcomes related to tool use, this can be a way to integrate those into the challenges. Having students figure out how to use a protractor, a compass, or learn about the properties of a prism so they are able to solve a puzzle can be enjoyable activities in a game format, as the students will be the ones to make the connections about how the tools work instead of being told how they work by an instructor. An observational puzzle can also provide the 'a-ha' moment at the end of a puzzle sequence. Once the players have completed the skill element, they may have drawn something, or ordered something that reveals a pattern, a code, or instruction.

It can be important to provide guidance to help players with observational puzzles. When you create an observational puzzle, it will seem to you that the correct answer is obvious. But when the players are involved in a game, they are surrounded by potential patterns, components, and things that could be puzzles. Everything is new to them, so they can struggle to find the signal in the noise. Doing things like partially solving a puzzle, writing up guidance from an ally in a note, including a photograph of game elements put together in a certain way can help nudge the players. If you want to allow the players a chance to figure it all out on their own, then these types of hints can be delivered after a certain amount of time has passed to help the players stay on schedule to complete the game.

LOGIC PUZZLES

In a logic puzzle, the players are given a set of elements and a set of rules about those elements, with the goal of figuring out the one combination of elements that satisfies the rules. These puzzles can take many forms, for example:

- Putting things in order, such as determining what steps to take first in a process or recreating someone's day of activities.
- Matching up items from different categories, such as connecting people, places, and events (also known as an 'Einstein puzzle').
- Selecting a subset of items from a larger group, such as buildings on maps or books from a collection.

To start, select the affordances in the setting, world, and narrative that will make sense for the learning outcomes. In an escape game, it is usually better if there is some type of physical representation for the elements of the puzzle, but this type of puzzle can also be done with pencil and paper. For an example, we will use a learning outcome related to learning the different types of gases. Our setting is in a factory, and we need to figure out which combination of natural gases are used so we can repair the damage that has been done by a saboteur. For physical elements, we can create index cards that have the information about each of the gases.

The next step is to create the set of elements and the categories for the elements. When designing the puzzle, it can be useful to create a table with this information (see Table 6.2). For the elements of the puzzle, we have the name of the gas, if it is an artificial or natural gas, if it is an elemental or compound gas, the odor of the gas, the density of the gas, and what type of flammability the gas has.

Table 6.2 Information about gases

Name	Type	Odor	Density	Flammability
Hydrogen	Elemental	None	.09	Flammable
Oxygen	Elemental	None	1.4	Oxidizer
Nitrogen	Elemental	None	1.2	Inert
Helium	Elemental	None	.17	Inert
Sulfur Dioxide	Compound	Burnt matches	2.8	Inert
Carbon Dioxide	Compound	Acid (high concentrations)	1.9	Inert
Methane	Compound	None	.7	Flammable
Chlorine	Compound	Bleach	3.1	Oxidizer

Table 6.2 would not be given to the players, but the players may be given objects to represent each item that has symbols or data from the table, which might also be a learning outcome (to understand how to read warning and informational labels on chemicals). Another learning outcome could be to not give the players complete information, but instead to expect them to do research to learn some of the above information. Spreading out the information in different sources will require the team to communicate and will increase the number of learning opportunities.

The next step is to determine the task and the correct solution to the task. In this case, the task might be to select the three correct gases and put them in the correct order (which will need to be communicated to the players). If each gas is numbered, then that creates a three-digit code which could open a lock in the game.

At this point in the design process, it is useful to look at the data for patterns that might lead to interesting clues. There are three different types of flammability, so that leads nicely to an answer set that requires one inert gas, one oxidizer, and one flammable gas. Each category provides a different way to divide the set of elements into groups – elemental vs. compound, odor vs. no odor, and density above, below, or the same as the density of air (which is 1.2). Note that the density of air is not in the table, and for a recreational escape room, that information would need to be provided in some way. For an educational game, this could require the players to research to learn this fact or expect that they already know it if this game is reviewing/assessing existing knowledge.

The goal is to create four to six clues that will allow the players to come up with the single answer that satisfies all of the clues. The clues typically take one of three forms:

- 'Yes' clues, which provide part of the answer. (Oxygen is required.)
- 'No' clues, which eliminate an element from the answer. (There is no gas lighter than air included.)
- 'Choose one' clues, which provide multiple possibilities, each of which need to be tested. (There are two elemental gases and one compound gas.)

'Yes' clues are the easiest clues to process and provide a starting point for solving, so it is good to start with a single 'yes' clue in the list of clues. It does not need to be first, but gives the players that first step in the right direction once they find it. 'No' clues are also easy to process but do not provide as much direction; they are useful near the end of the design process to close off possible solutions. 'Yes' and 'No' clues can also eliminate categories of elements, which might be useful when creating an easier puzzle.

The 'choose one' clues are where logic puzzles are most interesting and challenging, and should be the bulk of the clues. These can be broad, such as our initial restriction that the final combination must contain one of each flammability type, or they can be very focused, such as there being either Methane or Chlorine, but not both. At first, it will be impossible to resolve the 'choose one' clues until other clues are resolved, and this is a key part of solving a logic puzzle – figuring out the order in which the clues can be applied. Challenging logic puzzles have several interlocking 'choose one' statements, each of which can be resolved only along with the resolution of other 'choose one' statements, and the players have to set up multiple hypothetical situations until they find the one that is right.

While it may be tempting to insert more data into the logic puzzle statements than is needed to boost the learning outcome, this can also introduce red herrings, which can be frustrating to the players. A statement like 'Chlorine gas, which is poisonous, is not required' may be interesting, but if the fact that Chlorine is poisonous is not needed for the puzzle, this can frustrate learners. If there is a learning outcome about which gases are poisonous, it should be a key part of the puzzle and not an extraneous fact placed in the puzzle.

Once you have developed the set of statements that lead to the correct solution, it is important to test all possibilities so that there is not a different answer that can also satisfy all the conditions. Start by applying all of your 'yes' and 'no' clues, and then identify the most restrictive 'choose one' clue. Write out the possible options for that 'choose one clue', and then apply the other 'choose one' clues (again, working with the more restrictive ones first) to each of those options. If you discover multiple solutions, then either add another 'no' clue or adjust a 'choose one' restriction to make it so only one solution is correct.

The next step is to consider how the players will learn if their solution is correct. The solution will resolve some type of gate in the game. If the gate is a code for a lock, then the players will need a clue or directions as to what order to convert the elements into the numbers for the locks. A directional lock could be used in this case following the directional lock example in Chapter 5. Some puzzle designers have a logic puzzle to determine a subset of elements, and then leave it for the players to guess at what order those elements go in for the lock. The puzzle should be in figuring out the answer, not in guessing what the final answer could be, so provide direction to the players as to how to sequence the answer. This is not important if you are using a digital form or a human facilitator where all of the elements are required, but the order is not needed.

With the list of clues in hand, the next step is to return to the setting, world, and narrative, and think about how to convey this information to the players. The least immersive method is to give the players a list of the clues and paper to work out the answer. This also encourages one person to take on the challenge, as there is not an easy way for the group to work together. The first task is to look at how to distribute the elements of the puzzle – having physical manifestations for each element, having information about the elements in different places or requiring online research will all create opportunities for teamwork on the puzzle.

The clues can also be distributed, rather than provided in a single list. By putting the clues on different index cards instead of a single list, it will allow the player to work together. The clues could also be posted at different positions around the room, which will then add a searching layer to the game and increase teamwork opportunities. By thinking about the affordances, there could be clues provided in the environment. In this example, rather than telling the players that they need to get one gas of each flammability type, there could be a physical holder for the physical representations of the gases, and the holder could have 'inert', 'oxidizer', and 'flammable' symbols on the slots. This then also solves the ordering issue from above if the number that each gas represents is on each representation, as the code will then be shown to the players on the physical representation.

There can also be clues built into the physical representation that could not be conveyed easily through words. If the physical representation for each of the elements is a certain shape, and the holder for the representations only allows for certain combinations of shapes, this creates a 'choose one' clue. For example, it could be that the physical representation of a molecule connects together like a jigsaw, but not all pieces fit with all other pieces. Another option would be a rectangular frame that the pieces fit into, so that not all pieces can work together. While this type of physical element can be fun for people that like tactile puzzles, it rarely conveys a learning outcome, so should be used as a single clue in a larger puzzle that does convey learning outcomes.

Refining Logic Puzzles

In general, the more clues that have to be simultaneously processed, the harder a logic puzzle is to solve. To make a logic puzzle easier, add more direct 'yes' or 'no' clues, or add an additional 'choose one' clue that removes more possibilities. It can also be made easier by giving the clues in an order that leads to the solution instead of requiring the players to figure out the best order in which to apply clues. The puzzle can be made easier by providing part of the answer to the players at the beginning, either by telling them something (which is a 'yes' clue), or by gluing some of the initial elements in place; conversely, it can be made more difficult by setting up the puzzle in a way that is misleading. For example, if pieces are to be connected in some way, starting the puzzle with pieces connected that don't belong together in the final solution can make it more difficult. Another way to increase the challenge is to remove 'yes' clues, or change them to 'no' clues, or provide fewer restrictions in the 'choose one' clues. Finally, more depth can be added to the puzzle by requiring the players to either search or do research to get all of the needed information about the elements or the clues.

DEDUCTION PUZZLES

Deduction puzzles are similar to logic puzzles, but the presentation and approach to solving them is different. Logic puzzles teach deductive reasoning with cold hard facts. There is a definitive right answer once all the clues and factors are taken into account. The players even know for certain how many clues are needed, and at what point they will have enough information for it to be solvable. Logic puzzles can be made, and solved, on a logic grid. While the ticks and crosses of logic puzzles engage the mind, they lose the richness that may be useful to helping to convey a narrative or learning outcome.

A deduction puzzle moves away from the pure strategy and process of deductive logic, and crosses into the narrative level of the game. As such, a deduction puzzle is more useful and usual in an educational game than in a commercial one. One of your learning outcomes may be that the players have to create a convincing argument as to who committed the murder. In that scenario, you may use a deduction puzzle to get the players to deduce a password for Mr. Brown's USB stick. You present the clues in the narrative, or they may be a mixture of narrative clues and puzzle pieces, cold hard facts and evidence, that the players piece together to discover that:

- Mr. Brown loves dogs.
- He moved into a flat that didn't permit dogs and so had to give his dog up.
- Mrs. Raven adopted a dog from a friend who couldn't look after it anymore.
- Mrs. Raven received a birthday card signed by Mr. Brown.

- Mrs. Raven's dog is called 'Smithy'.
- Therefore, Mr. Brown's password could be 'Smithy'.

It is a logical chain of thought that leads us to suppose that Mrs. Raven and Mr. Brown are friends because of the birthday card. One of them just lost a dog, one of them gained a dog. It could be the same dog. Mr. Brown loves dogs, so Mr. Brown would use his dog's name as his password, even though that dog now belonged to Mrs. Raven. The players try the dog's name as a password – and the USB stick whirrs into life.

Later on in the game, as containers are opened and evidence gathered, and secrets come to light, this same sort of deductive reasoning will be used by the teams as they argue the case for what they think really happened and then, between them, working at the social and collaborative level of the game, they come up with a solution to present to the class.

Hints for deduction puzzles are easy to create, because you can simply add other clues to the game until the players figure it out. They can be delivered in-character: a text message pings, a letter arrives, a printer bursts into life. If there are role-playing elements in the game, then the scripted character can just be gossiping with the players and dropping hints until they hear the sharp intake of breath that signals a realization. In fact, deduction puzzles are important for many live-action role-playing games – the players are working to solve the plot, understand motivations and stay one step ahead of the bad guys using memetic clues in the dialogue.

Deduction puzzles can also be presented as cliffhangers or 'what happened next?' questions that are wonderful for raising excitement in the class, and letting the players play with the story. Whether it's fact or fiction, they can get curious about what really happened and even whether their version of events is better. They work well with game shapes where each team only gets partial information and have to negotiate with other teams to fill in the missing pieces, or in serial story games where the players have a while to mull over solutions, and will supplement their cogitations with some research between classes.

> Examine this building, marked on a map with an O. Why did it catch fire? Why did the fire travel so quickly? What six-letter substance was the main contributing factor? (Did you get Oxygen? The O is a visual clue connecting the word to the map.)

These puzzles are deeply satisfying to solve. They make the players feel so clever, like Sherlock Holmes, precisely because there is a leap of intuition needed, however small, once all the information has been synthesized. You can take inspiration from any film where the plot twist, the bait and switch, the setup and payback are all revealed by the application of deductive reasoning. Creating deduction puzzles and using the narrative as a metapuzzle makes your players pay attention and get involved in the story. They have to read it, and crucially for English comprehension, understand it. It also gives them opportunity to demonstrate their information handling skills.

MATH PUZZLES

In recreational escape rooms, math-based puzzles are common. Some types of math puzzles seen in escape rooms include:

- Figuring out what numbers replace letters in a problem, such as ME+ME=BEE.
- Determining the weight of different objects portrayed on balanced scales.
- Calculating the value of items purchased in different combinations when you only know the total of each purchase.
- Measuring out a volume of water or sand using several buckets of different known volumes.
- Determining how many days passed between two dates.

For educational escape games, math puzzles should only be used when the mathematics is needed for the desired learning outcomes. While these puzzles can be enjoyable for some, as each puzzle is an opportunity to connect to learning outcomes, using a math puzzle when there are no math-based learning outcomes wastes one of these opportunities.

Because math puzzles in educational escape games are based on specific learning outcomes, we will not be talking about the wide spectrum of math concepts in this book. Instructors that are teaching mathematical concepts already have math-based challenges that they use in their traditional classrooms. Therefore, to create a math-based challenge in an educational escape game, instructors should start with math problems that reinforce the learning outcomes.

The mistake is when instructors include a math problem in an escape game as only a math problem. If the players are traveling through the Tomb of the Lost Wizard, and the Ghouly Ghost appears and asks them to, 'Solve X, Y, and Z in this set of equations and use the answer to open this padlock', it is not going to be a narrative-based experience. Instead, it will feel to the students as though the instructor is just having them do math worksheets in a different form.

As escape games can be simulations, they provide a good setting for an instructor to help students understand the real-world applications of what they are learning in the classroom. Word problems that demonstrate real-world applications for math like the example on page 65, help students understand the genuine value of what they are learning. Since escape games allow for physical props, for multiple forms of information (such as maps, blueprints, catalogs, or reference books), and for the development of a storyworld and setting with constraints and affordances, then these games can allow for the realization of the real-world importance of their mathematical skills.

If the learning outcomes are math-based, then it is important to select a setting and a narrative that will support the real-world application of the math skills. If there is no real-world setting where the math-based learning outcomes make sense, then escape games are not the best tool for exploring those learning outcomes. Escape games are also not very good to support math drills, where students are doing the same type of problems again and again to learn a technique. In both of these situations, more traditional teaching forms like worksheets will be a better use of classroom time. Escape games are better used to help students realize the importance of what they are learning, either by having them explore the concepts before formally learning them in the classroom, or by having them demonstrate competency of using the concepts in an applied setting.

In the sample game, the 'Graph Grifting' puzzle is a math-based puzzle that is firmly grounded in the real-world application of reading graphs that are designed to be misleading. By using a real-world situation for the math application, it helps the learner understand why the underlying math skills are important. In this case, after solving this puzzle, players will be more likely to take a second look at visual data to make sure there isn't something misleading going on.

To make a math-based challenge easier, it can be useful to supply the players with an already-solved problem that is similar that they can analyze. If the players have an ally or are following the trail of someone who has already been in the space, then it might make narrative sense that they see how someone else worked out a similar problem. Another technique would be to show how this person worked out the problem incorrectly, and it is up to the players to figure out what went wrong. Yet another approach to helping players would be to have the problem partially solved, so that the players are able to continue from where someone left off.

Another way to make the problem easier is to document common mistakes that could be made when solving it. If there is a case where people forget to use the order of operations, for example, then have a note that the players encounter at the correct point, which is a reminder someone left to themselves about remembering the order of operations. If there is a common incorrect path that leads to a specific wrong answer, there could be an already worked-out answer that is crossed out, indicating that is not the correct path. Only by playtesting will the designer be able to understand where the common pitfalls lie, and decide if those are to be part of the challenge, or if they create too much of a challenge and need to be addressed.

If the math-based challenge is too easy, then removing information is the best way to make it more difficult. It may be tempting to create red herrings and add additional incorrect information, but this can be very frustrating for players who then work through solving problems based on incorrect information. A player who starts with incorrect or misleading data, goes to the trouble of solving the problem, only to learn their answer is wrong because they were being 'tricked', will be less likely to trust the designer of the game and will disengage from the activity. It is better to not provide key information that has to be discovered through another challenge, and part of the learning from this activity is realizing what is needed before a technique can be applied.

CRYPTOGRAPHY

Coded messages are a cornerstone activity for recreational escape rooms. They are easy to create, can convey a genre and narrative elements, and are inexpensive puzzles to prototype. As such, they are tempting tools to use in creating an educational escape game; however, we need to remember our focus on the learning outcomes. Every minute the players are working through a decryption process for fun is a minute of the game they are not pursuing the learning outcomes. There may be learning outcomes that could be adapted to cryptography, such as foreign languages, learning symbols or abbreviations, or mathematics, but for most learning outcomes, cryptography based tasks are a distraction from the learning goals of the game.

That said, there are times in games where using light cryptography tasks would be appropriate. Some genres, such as espionage, rely on secret messages to help immerse the players in the role of being a spy. Narratives where someone has left behind messages for the players are perfect times to introduce cryptography-based tasks. In these cases, the cryptography challenge should be easy and not take much time; the real focus and challenge of the game should be on activities that bring about the learning outcomes.

Where cryptography works well in educational escape games is as a gating tool. While padlocks and sealed envelopes can keep content hidden away until it is time, cryptography allows the content to be in plain sight. Having a mysterious note, unusual strip of paper with letters on it, or blank sheet of paper included with other materials, engages players and raises curiosity. Then, when another challenge rewards players with the 'key' to the secret message, the players can then open up that gated content and continue with the game. The challenge should not be in decrypting the message; the challenge should be in the task based on the learning outcome that then leads the players to the key that lets them decrypt the message. The decryption should be an engaging task that reveals secrets, but not an onerous one.

The core concept of cryptography is that a message is hidden in some way that requires some information or a process to recover it. In this book, we are only going to discuss a few of these basic methods as the goal of using cryptography in an educational escape game is as a gate for content, not for a challenge of decoding something with a complex method. In this chapter, we focus on ciphers and codes as two forms of cryptography, where ciphers focus on the swapping of individual letters, while codes substitute entire words or concepts for replacements.

Ciphers and Codes

A cipher is a tool that converts letters into something else. In a classical substitution cipher, each letter is substituted for another letter. In the Caesar substitution cipher, this is done by shifting all of the letters forward by a number of letters in the alphabet.

So, if that number is five, then A would become (b c d e) F, and B would become G, and so on. Once the players figure out what the mystery number is, they can easily translate the entire message. The substitutions could also be made in other ways, such as reversing the alphabet so that A becomes Z, and Z becomes A or randomly mixing up all of the letters, thus making it harder to break. With any substitution cipher, if the substitution rule has been consistently followed, then the players have the ability to crack the code if they have a long piece of text to discover letter patterns.

Another common cipher is the letter–number cipher, where each letter is replaced by a number. In the A1Z26 cipher, the letter A is replaced by 1, while the letter Z is replaced by 26. As above, to make this more difficult to break without the key, randomize the numbers for each letter. A version of this letter–number cipher, called a Polybius square uses a 5 × 5 square for 25 of the letters (omitting one unused letter) with numbered rows and columns, as seen in Table 6.3. The row and column numbers are used to replace the letters, so '42' would be Q.

Table 6.3 Example of Polybius square cipher tool

	1	**2**	**3**	**4**	**5**
1	A	B	C	D	E
2	F	G	H	I	J
3	K	L	M	N	O
4	P	Q	R	S	T
5	U	V	W	Y	Z

There are other well-known ciphers that can be easily implemented. Braille, Morse code, and semaphore (using flags to represent letters) are all commonplace in recreational escape rooms. For any of these schemes, it is important to provide the players with the key or expect that part of the challenge is that they will have to find a key online. To make these challenges more interesting, there are creative ways to present the message that are not print-based. For example, a Braille representation can be created with toy building blocks or large bumps attached under a table so that the players actually have to feel the Braille with their hand to translate it. Morse code can be communicated through sound (although decoding Morse code by sound under time pressure can be challenging) or through a blinking light. Semaphore can be communicated through the hands of clocks. Being too tricky in delivering the code, however, can leave your players frustrated. For all of these well-known schemes, an easy way to create a paper-based version of the challenge is to download a font for the code, type in your message, and then change the font to the cipher-based font.

The difference between codes and ciphers is that ciphers are focused on encoding individual letters while codes are focused on encoding entire words or concepts. A common code in recreational escape rooms is a book code. In a book code, the players are given a series of page, line, and word numbers and a book. By looking up each word in the book, it will lead to a message. Another coding system is American Sign Language, where different hand gestures turn into different words or concepts. Foreign languages could also be seen as a coding scheme, as they are translated at the word/concept level instead of letter by letter. Therefore, based upon the learning outcome, a coding scheme may be more appropriate to use than a cipher.

One caveat in presenting a message that uses a common cipher scheme is that players may be able to figure out the message ahead of time. Students may already know Morse code, Braille, or the standard A1Z26 encoding scheme, and can take the message and crack the code. When you design the game, you need to decide if this is problematic. One way to deal with this problem is to not provide all of the message to be decoded up front, but instead, provide some of the message with the key. The clever student can decrypt some of the message, but only when they find the key with the critical elements of the message can they open that gate. Another technique is to make the encoded message only part of what is needed to overcome the next gate, and it must be combined with a result from a different task to move on. Conversely, if it will not cause a gameplay problem, then you can let the clever players be clever and access more of the game ahead of time.

ROLE-PLAYING CHALLENGES

In a role-playing challenge, the players have an opportunity to become more immersed in the game by being required to engage socially or make decisions based upon the narrative. While puzzle-based challenges allow the players to stand at arm's length and engage in the game activities, role-playing challenges require a deeper level of engagement. Because of this, some players can be uncomfortable and unwilling to participate in a role-playing challenge. That said, there are learning outcomes for which a role-playing challenge will be the best way to help players reach these outcomes. Any learning outcome that is based on students exploring different points of view, developing empathy, or understanding the 'why' behind the 'what' could benefit from a role-playing challenge.

There are three dimensions to explore when developing a role-playing challenge. It can be best to think of each as a slider instead of a switch, as each dimension can be incorporated at different levels. This concept is more fully explored in the Mixing Deck of LARP, which conceptualized a set of sliders for designing live-action role-playing games (Stenros et al., 2016).

Playing Themselves–Playing a Character

The first dimension is the amount to which the player is asked to take on a character in the world. On one side of this dimension, the players are themselves in an unusual situation, and players are not told who they are in the world, and they just happened to be in the wrong place at the wrong time. Slightly more immersive than this is where the players are given a role, such as 'You are a detective', but no other world or narrative information is provided. Going further down this dimension, players could be given a role and provided with some types of tools, costume pieces, or information that helps them act out that role. For example, the player could be an investigator, and are provided with a toolkit with a magnifying glass, a scope to see in small places, a Morse code translation table, and a Sherlock Holmes hat. Having these physical accessories allows players to 'role play' more in the challenge. While these tools could be provided during the course of the game, giving them to the players at the start makes it easier for the player to immerse themselves in the role by helping them transition from the real world into the game world.

On the other side of this dimension is where the player is not playing themselves, but instead playing a character in the world. To do this, the player will need a briefing explaining who they are, what their goals are in the world, previous knowledge about the world and the incidents that have taken place, and key moments from the past that help them understand their relationship with allies and enemies in the game. When creating a backstory for a player, it is important to focus just on those things that are needed for the game; while you could provide a much longer backstory to read, this will be too overwhelming for most players. Providing a set of brief statements with key people, places, and concepts in bold will help the player understand the role they are playing.

The decision about how much backstory to provide a player should be driven by the learning outcomes. In a history or literature class, there may be learning outcomes focused on understanding specific people and their role in the narrative, so giving players those roles will be one way to address that learning outcome. It can be more meaningful for a player to take on a historical role and have a game that demonstrates the impact of making different decisions instead of playing the ally who is the assistant to someone important.

Using Items–Using Information

The next dimension to consider is how the players will overcome the role-playing challenges. The typical player loop in a role-playing challenge is that a non-player character wants something, and in exchange will provide the player with what they need for the next step in overcoming the next gate. One way this can be accomplished in the game is through challenges involving items that the player has acquired. In this type of challenge, the player needs to learn about the motivations and goals of the non-player character enough to know what item they would like in order to let the player continue. This could be an observational puzzle, where the player sees food stains on the front of a guard's costume, so can figure out that bribing the guard with food might be successful, or could be a research puzzle, where the player has learned ahead of time what types of things are desirable to someone in a trading situation. In an item-based role-playing challenge, the player is not usually expected to talk much; they simply hand over the correct item to the non-player character and are rewarded.

On the other side of this dimension are challenges that are about the exchange of information. This type of challenge is all about talking, where the players may have some information and need to determine what the non-player character is needing to know. The players probably have much more information than is needed in the situation, so will have to learn about the non-player character's situation in the narrative in order to know what to say (and what not to say). This type of challenge is valuable when the learning outcome is about building empathy or understanding the different perspectives of people in a situation. To help players struggling with this type of challenge, the ally of the players could provide them with notecards with questions that the players could ask the non-player character.

Blending these two concepts can create challenges where the players have space for creativity. Players may have both items and information, and can use them together to overcome the role-playing challenge. The core challenge is still the same – the players need to understand what the desires are of this non-player character and what they value or fear, and then use their own items and information to accomplish their goals. For example, the player could meet up with a hired mercenary who is working for a king, but doing so because the king has threatened his lands if he doesn't work for the crown. If the players have researched and understood this situation, they could come up with a number of valid solutions to get the mercenary to let down his guard and let the players pass by. In these types of situations, it can be important in the design to be flexible with what solutions will work to succeed at the challenge in order to allow the space for creative players to succeed.

Same Roles–Different Roles

The final dimension we will explore here is based upon the roles that the players are asked to take on for the game. The most straightforward version of this is when the players are all in the same role. For example, in the example above, the players are all investigators and they share one toolkit that has a number of items in it, and enough identical costume pieces for everyone to play dress-up. If there is a background narrative, it will usually be read out loud, either by the facilitator or by the players, and the focus is on a fully cooperative game.

Moving one step away from the same roles is the concept of different roles, but on the same team. In this situation, each player is provided with a different role and has information, tools, or accessories that make them different from the other players, but they have a shared goal. In the investigator example, there could be someone who is the forensics expert and has fingerprint powder and instructions on how to use it, while someone else is communications, and has a walkie-talkie and Morse code, and a third player is the technician, and has the UV light and camera. This type of item-based role playing makes it easier for shy students to take on a role, as it creates game moments where they can step forward to be the hero as they have the tool that is needed in the situation.

The same concept can be used with information, where each player has their own backstory and information about the world, and non-player characters. The difficulty with implementing the concept is that it puts significant pressure on one player to remember something at a key moment. With the item-based role playing, the other team members can see what each player has, so if a player forgets they have something, a team member can remind them. But with information-based role playing, the same visual clues are not available. This might require extra prompting to be written into the game, where information requests are directed at the player who has the specific information needed.

On the other end of the spectrum is where the players are not working toward the same goal. They may be required to cooperate, as they can't reach their own goal by themselves, but at some point there will be conflict between players when a choice has to be made. This type of scenario is very useful in any learning outcome that is designed to show conflict, as it will put the players in the roles of the different sides represented in the conflict. This type of game can get quite competitive, so should only be used when it is important to demonstrate a real-world conflict.

This concept can also be useful in a multi-team game, where different teams are playing the game at the same time. It could be that each team is made up of people playing different roles, and the teams are competing to be the first to accomplish the challenge. Or each team could have a different overall goal, and the purpose of the game is to have the players explore negotiation and compromise between different factions. Yet another model would have players divided into different groups, and then teams are created from one player from each group to explore the tensions between different roles people play in society. Going beyond puzzles by incorporating role-playing challenges allows for the exploration of complex situations that would be difficult to explore using traditional paper-based techniques in the classroom.

METAPUZZLES

Metapuzzles are puzzles that bring together elements from previous puzzles, requiring the previous puzzles to be solved before the metapuzzle can be solved. Traditionally, they are used in non-linear game designs where players can work on multiple puzzles at once. Answers from each of the individual puzzles are brought together to complete the metapuzzle. The metapuzzle serves as a gate to ensure that the players have completed all of the smaller puzzles before moving on to a new part of the game. A common metapuzzle using a single four-digit lock is that there is a process for the answer to each of four individual puzzles to be converted into a single digit, and then each digit makes up one digit of the four-digit combination. Conceptually, the players need to work through each of the four puzzles to get the four answers needed to find the four digits, and this helps the designer control the narrative and delivery of challenges to the players.

In educational escape games, the metapuzzles can serve another role, and that is one of reflection. Some metapuzzles have the players return to earlier solved puzzles to look at them in a different way and bring forth new information for the metapuzzle. For example, if there were a series of individual puzzles about electrical circuits where players planned out different devices, a metapuzzle could introduce the threat of water and provide new resources to the player to waterproof their circuits, and require the players to return to each puzzle to see how they could be waterproofed. In this way, a metapuzzle can be used in a linear game design, where the team works on each puzzle together. The metapuzzle would add a non-linear element to the linear design, as the players could split up to work on the revisions to the original puzzles. Therefore, metapuzzles should be considered when there is a reflection-based activity that would lead to the learning outcomes.

The biggest challenge with using a metapuzzle is that, based upon their design, they can enable players to skip the individual puzzles. In the example above with the four-digit padlock, once players have solved three of the puzzles, they could just roll the tumbler for the fourth digit until the lock opens. This would allow them to bypass one of the puzzles, which could be problematic if each puzzle is designed to focus on a different learning outcome. It can also make players feel cheated out of an experience, as many teams will skip doing the individual puzzles if there is time pressure to complete the game as quickly as possible.

There are two ways to overcome this problem. The first is to not allow access to the metapuzzle until all of the individual puzzles are completed. This could be done by a facilitator holding the metapuzzle, and a team comes up to show they have completed all of the previous puzzles before they are given the metapuzzle. Another is through clever design: instead of having each puzzle resolve to a single digit number, some of the puzzles resolve to numbers with more digits. Then, to solve the metapuzzle, the players have to add together the answers from the individual puzzles. This creates an answer that is much more difficult to guess from only three of the puzzles. In the sample game in Part 3, the 'Fingerprint' metapuzzle requires all three parts of information to identify the specific fingerprint. However, a weakness of this puzzle is that with two of the pieces of information, the players can narrow the possibilities down to a small subset of possible answers, so that if they had a four-digit padlock to resolve the puzzle, it would be easy to try all of the solutions.

REFERENCES

Stenros, J., Andresen, M., and Nielsen, M. (2016) The Mixing Desk of LARP: History and Current State of a Design Theory, *Analog Game Studies*. Available online at http://analoggamestudies.org/2016/11/the-mixing-desk-of-larp-history-and-current-state-of-a-design-theory/.

7 DESIGNING THE ESCAPE GAME EXPERIENCE

By this time in your game design, you have learning outcomes, a world, a narrative, and a set of challenges that are built around those learning outcomes. The next challenge is how to put all of these together into a cohesive game. Skipping this step may result in an activity that will feel like a random assortment of puzzles. To use a meal metaphor, this is the difference between having a planned five-course dinner presented to you, one course at a time, or being turned loose at a buffet where the same dishes are all presented at once. You'll get the same food, but you'll have a different experience.

Many of these concepts are about experience design. They are models from different fields, but all focused on the same idea – how to create a better experience for your players. As a game designer, you create structures and spaces for your players to explore, but they will end up crafting their own engagement. Some players will be more interested in the world, others interested in the story, others will want to work as a team, others just want to do the puzzles, and some people will not be engaged in what you create.

As you learn more about game design, you will discover that there are conflicting models of how to present activities. In this chapter, we present different ways to think about how to combine your puzzles into a game, and each method may lead to a different result. It can be useful to think of each model as a gameplay advisor; you can listen to each one, but at the end you'll have to make the decision as to what makes the most sense for your narrative, audience, and the experience you want to create.

GATING CONTENT

One of the most important tools an escape game creator has to control the experience for the players is the ability to create gates. A gate is a point in the game where the players cannot continue until they find the way to pass the gate. If the escape game is designed with ten challenges, then if all ten challenges are presented to the player at once, it will be overwhelming. Gates allow the designer to reduce the number of activities that are available to the player at any one time in order to control the player experience so that teams are only faced with a few challenges at a time.

These gates could be physical gates, such as boxes with padlocks or sealed envelopes. They could also be mental gates, such as an encrypted message for which the players do not yet have the encoding scheme. Some gates require the players to combine items they have discovered, such as wrapping a ribbon with letters around a stick to reveal a message or using a special UV flashlight to reveal hidden messages. Clever players may figure out ways around gates ahead of time, which can end up creating a bad player experience for the team.

In recreational escape room design, there are different models for using gates to control content. In a linear game, the challenges are presented to the players one at a time. Each one has a gate, so completing one challenge will then make the next challenge available to the players. In a non-linear game, multiple challenges are available to the players all at once, and after all are solved, then there is a gate to allow the players to continue. This gate is a metapuzzle that requires the successful completion of the individual puzzles. For example, in Breakout EDU, this metapuzzle gate is commonly implemented as a hasp that can hold multiple locks (see Figure 7.1). Each puzzle leads to one lock, and when all of the locks are open, the players can continue.

Most recreational games use a hybrid model, where players will have a few puzzles available to them at the start of the room. There may be some puzzle paths, where one puzzle leads to another, and some puzzles will be on their own. The result of solving all of the puzzles in the room will give the players the 'keys' needed to unlock the gate to the next room.

The problem with these non-linear models in educational escape games is that not all players will encounter all of the activities in the room. In non-linear rooms, they are typically designed so that the players will divide up the tasks, and people can work on something they enjoy. If there is a math puzzle and a word puzzle available at the same time, then players who enjoy math can avoid the word puzzle and vice versa. The resulting player experience is more enjoyable for most people, as they were able to focus on what they liked doing. In an educational game, the purpose of the challenges is to move the players toward the learning outcomes. If the players are able to split up and work on different challenges, then an individual player will not be able to engage with each step of the process and may miss some of the development.

Therefore, it is recommended that educational escape games use a linear model, where the entire team will engage with each challenge together. If there are multiple

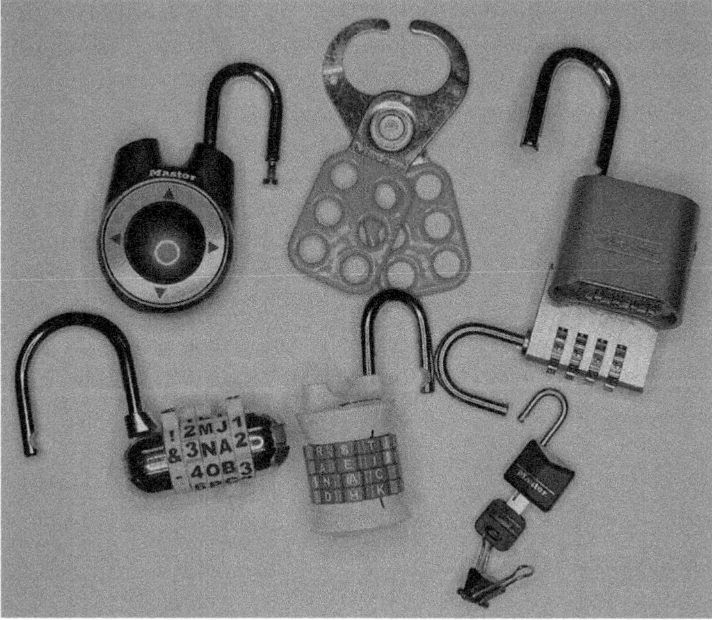

Figure 7.1 Opened hasp with directional lock, five-dial letter/number lock (interchangeable rings), four-dial letter lock (fixed), key lock with binder clip on key to avoid loss, and two different styles of four-digit numerical locks

challenges available, they should be designed to provide similar experiences, so that as long as a player was engaged with one of the challenges, they were able to move closer to the learning outcomes. If it is better for the game design to have students working on different activities at the same time, then it is important to include some type of sharing activity as part of the game.

It is also important to consider the location of information and components for puzzles in relationship to the gates they unlock. Players do not know what will help them open a gate, so everything they have access to is potentially part of the solution. It is very easy to accidentally create red herrings for players by putting information or puzzle components too early in the game, as the players will be thinking, 'This object is here for a reason'. As part of designing a good game experience, consider carefully at what stage of the game you provide things to players to help them not get confused.

CONTAINERS AND GATES

An escape game is essentially a series of locked containers that need unlocking by the players so that the containers can be opened and reveal further puzzles to solve. These containers hold the content, while the locks are the gates that prevent progress. Locks were discussed earlier in the book in relation to puzzle design; Table 5.1 lists common locks and considerations.

The most common containers in escape games are some type of box that has the ability to be held closed with a padlock. There are many plastic, metal, and wood boxes that can hold locks, and inexpensive hasps can be purchased at the hardware store to add a metal loop to hold the padlock. It can be useful to find locks that have a cable instead of a shackle (like a soft bicycle lock) for more flexibility in securing containers. Cardboard boxes with lids also work well; these can be modified by either adding a hole that runs through the lid and side of the box for a lock, or by adding holes below the lid on both sides of the box and using cable-ties, a length of light chain, or a string with loops on either end to hold the padlock, as shown in Figure 7.2.

Figure 7.2 Adding a lock to a cardboard box

Many bags, pouches, and purses can also be modified to add a small padlock. Envelopes also work as containers and are easy to modify with a hole to add a padlock, although you may want to reinforce these holes with tape, so that the padlock doesn't rip through the envelopes. It can be worthwhile to mention to players at the start of the game to play within the spirit of the game; even though they could destroy the container or pry open the lid to get at the contents, they should open the lock before opening the container.

Locations as Containers

A container does not have to be small; the room that the game is in is itself a container, as are other physical spaces, such as closets, desks, or other rooms. You may not be able to physically lock the doors, but you can surprise the players by giving them instructions to go elsewhere at some point in the game, and so introduce a whole new location. This can introduce an element of communication if only one or two of the team members can go to the new location to observe something, and then report back to the rest of the team. In a round robin game shape, the students might take turns to visit the location as one of their stations. If there are computers or tablets available, you can create a virtual location with a small video, a panoramic photo, or a slide show of pictures of another room that you set up and took pictures of for the players to 'visit'.

Hidden Elements

You can make the most of your environment by hiding puzzles, containers, tools, and clues around the room. However, although this is a major part of commercial games, it is not so useful in an education context, except perhaps for the social element of the game and to emphasize teamwork. All the time the players are searching, they aren't learning or applying their learning. In addition, if there are multiple teams searching for the same thing in a space, once one team finds it, the others can just watch that team to find it. As searching can be frustrating, make it obvious what needs to be searched for, and make it relatively easy to find. Even sticking something to the underneath of a box, a wastebin, the table they are working on, can take them an inordinately long time to find, during which they can do nothing else or, worse, may attempt to go further without even having all the information and elements they need to solve the puzzle. If you do choose to hide elements, make sure you give an obvious cue or clue at the right point in the game that it is needed to pretty much guarantee that it will be found ('Have you looked under the table?'), but as it may be found earlier in the game by the extra-inquisitive team member, it needs to be something that won't make a difference if it is found earlier than it is needed in the narrative.

Books as Containers

Books are containers of information and can be important components in supporting learning outcomes. In recreational escape rooms, books are generally not appreciated as being parts of games, as they are typically used for tedious searching challenges (such as finding the correct book in a bookshelf), and get ragged quite quickly through thousands of plays. For educational escape games, however, books can make sense as a tool for the game as they are part of the educational goals.

To reach learning goals with books, the books need to be used in the way that students would use them outside of the game. The players can be given challenges that simulate the real world and will then use the books to find the answers to the challenges. If this uses the class textbook, then all of the students can work on the challenges at the same time. It also can be useful to require the students to locate a reference book in the room and use it, as this is teaching the students where to find this book in the future. The closer that you can map the challenge to a real-world situation, the more likely it is that the simulation will prepare people for reality.

Books can also be used as giant look-up tables or word references to add a layer to another challenge. The answers to several different puzzles could provide players with a page number, a line number, and a word on that line, and that word could then be the password that is whispered in the facilitator's ear or entered into a padlock. The players could have a 'mask', which is an overlay with holes in it, or a transparency with markings on it, and when the mask is laid on top of a specific page, a message shows through. (Side note: this type of masking works with any type of printed material, such as newspapers, calendars or letters.)

The information from a specific page could be a hint or guidance for another puzzlc. For cxamplc, thc book could show a diagram of how to assemble a pendulum. The players then put their own pendulum together using the diagram, and then find when they swing it, the pendulum stops at a specific point over the base (because you've put a magnet in the pendulum and another magnet in the base).

Finally, the book itself could be a container. You can cut out the center of pages in the book and use glue on the rectangles left behind after cutting them to create a hollowed-out book. The book can hold a book mark, a plane ticket, a pressed flower, or anything flat as a hiding place queued by a hint left by an ally. The information (such as the title) on the outside of one or more books could be used as a clue or an answer to a challenge.

One warning about relying upon books for a game – as previously mentioned, books get damaged quite easily when handled roughly. If you are looking to replace a book and use a different edition than the one you built the game around, you may find that page number and word references now no longer work, so you'll need to verify that all of your book puzzles still work when replacing your books.

ADDING ENVIRONMENTAL STORYTELLING

Back in Chapter 3, we explored creating the world and setting for the game. It is at this point where you should consider how you will convey that world to the players through environmental storytelling. We have been talking about placing objects in the environment, but what is that environment? If you have matched the environment for the game with the actual environment (such as the library for a game set in the library), then you are further ahead, but you still have some work to do. Set dressing, characterization, special effects, and soundtracks are not extraneous extras. Learning is optimized when learners are interested and engaged with the content to be mastered. This seductive augmentation, which involves the addition of graphics, sound, music, or video, improves engagement, and therefore learning, even when it is either irrelevant or only slightly relevant to the learning objectives. Narrative theming, and the addition of exciting elements such as black lights, dry ice, and laser mazes do therefore have pedagogical purpose, when used in moderation.

Here is a checklist of things to consider to add environmental storytelling to your game:

- Lighting: while it might be easy to make the room dark, this can also make it difficult for your players to read their challenges. If you lower the room lights, you will need to provide the players with lighting at their stations. If you are going to require the players to use flashlights, make sure there is one flashlight per person; it is incredibly frustrating to be sitting in the dark with nothing to do because you don't have a light source. Depending upon the types of fixtures in the room, you could add colored filters or replace the bulbs with colored bulbs to change the mood. If you have a theater department, they may have lights you could borrow to change the mood. (Note: while multicolored LED smart bulbs would give you considerable flexibility, they typically need to connect to a Wi-Fi network to function, and many school's Wi-Fi networks are locked down, so they won't work.)

- Posters: posters are a great way to add both environment and storytelling! You can also put puzzle content in the posters so that the players will need to move around the room to play the game. Be careful not to add red herrings with information on the posters; for example, if you are using a four-digit lock and it's not clear where the digits come from, players will enter every year they can find on these posters into the lock.
- Other room decorations: adding other elements to the room that are or are not part of challenges can immerse players. A visit to a thrift shop may be useful in helping you find a few items to help turn your classroom in a laboratory, dentist's office, or field laboratory. This might also be a time to visit your theater department or other departments in your school related to the environment for the game to find some props. As with the posters, be careful not to add anything that may mislead the players. This is the type of thing you might not realize until you run the game, as you usually playtest with just the puzzles and not a completed environment.
- Small props: it can be nice to have hand-held props that the players can fiddle with at their stations. A 3D printer or laser cutter can work well to help you craft challenge components that take it beyond drawings on sheets of paper. One warning – be careful to hide well away your supplies of locks and boxes for creating these games; we have had situations where players, during a deep search, came across these hidden locks, and brought them into the game, sowing much confusion.
- Audio: there are two kinds of audio to consider. The first is music that sets a tone for the game. You can use movie soundtracks as audio to get people into the mood, and that can also work as a timer for you to know when groups should be at a certain point in the game. Then, there is audio that would actually be heard at the scene, such as the ongoing sound of the engines and the water if the players are on a ship or the noise of hospital machines if they are in an emergency room. Both types of sounds are useful to add ambience. Using audio clues and puzzles in games can be frustrating in large-group situations because of the noise created by a classroom of excited students. If you wish to use an audio puzzle, the players should have their own speaker or headphone to be able to play the important audio over and over while they are solving the puzzle.
- Video: videos can be used in a few different ways. First, you can use a video as the introduction to the game. The advantage of this over a live presentation of

the introduction is that you can edit the video. You can film it in a setting that is important to the game, and you can edit the content to make sure that everything is covered. Second, the video can run the timer for the game, and this countdown clock could be spliced onto the video introduction so you are just pressing 'play' once. The audio soundtrack for the game can also be added into this timer video, so that there is one fewer item to worry about triggering on the day of the event. Finally, videos can be used during the game to update the players on changing situations. If the event is something that affects everyone, then it can be played on a large screen. If it is something that only is needed for a group, then you can either provide the group with a link or QR code to access the video, or create a 'viewing station' where the group can come and watch the video. In order to avoid people needing to rewatch the video (which could create a bottleneck for multiple teams) and to make the content more accessible, it can be good to have a written transcript of any audio or video content that can be delivered to the team after they see or hear the content.

- Costumes: adding a few costuming bits can really increase the immersion for both the players and yourself. Putting on a lab coat will help you transform from teacher to lab assistant. You can leave some costume pieces at the tables and encourage students to dress up. If you have specific roles assigned, then each role can come with a costume piece to wear. Another route is to let the students know ahead of time what the setting is for the game and invite them to wear costumes. Depending upon your setting, it might be interesting to have a 'costume making' session of the class before the escape room, so that players will do some research about the proper clothing and create an outfit they can then take home.

It is also useful to think about the pre-game ambience as students are filtering in the room. Most soundtracks by John Williams will help set a soundscape as the students come into the room and will raise the excitement level as the students know something is going on. When moving into reflection, it is important to turn the environmental effects off, as the goal is to take the players out of the game world and back into the real world, and another change in environment can help bring them out.

TIME LIMITS AND TANGIBLE REWARDS

Having 60 minutes to escape a room is a primary driver for players in commercial escape rooms. The core challenge is, 'Can you overcome these obstacles in the time limit?' However, as escape room players gain experience and become escape room enthusiasts, the focus on the clock fades away (until there are only a few minutes left), and many just enjoy exploring the space and puzzles with the confidence that if the game is fairly designed, they will be able to finish the game in time. Some, however, focus even more on the clock with the goal of breaking the time record for the room.

For these time-focused players, the game is not about enjoying the puzzles; the game is about finding any shortcut possible to achieve the goal of the game. Escape rooms companies are fine with this model, as faster and better teams require fewer staff resources.

Teachers new to using escape rooms in a classroom may be tempted to follow the same model as commercial escape rooms by focusing the game on the clock. This emphasis on time is increased if the game is presented as competitive between teams in the classroom. Even if there is no mention of the game being a competition between teams, some of the players will take it upon themselves to turn it into a race.

The problem with this focus on time is that it encourages the players to focus on the locks in the game instead of on the process to discover the key to open the lock. For example, if there is a word puzzle where there are certain blanks that are colored, and a lock that translates those colors into letters, then players have no incentive to solve any part of the puzzle that doesn't lead to a colored blank. If part of the learning outcome is explored through answering these questions, then those learning outcomes will not be reached through the game. If you use a three-digit padlock, but the challenge to get the three digits takes more time than it would take to manually try all of the combinations on the lock, then players racing for a fast solution will work through the combinations instead of doing the puzzle. Even if only one person is working with the lock, as soon as he or she gets it open, the rest of the team will then be demoralized and will not continue with the learning activity. Extending this concept, if there is a focus on which team finishes first, then once one team finishes the game, the other teams will be demoralized and may not even want to continue the game.

Recognizing this, there are some lessons to be applied when using escape games in the classroom. The first is to *de-emphasize the time limit*. While you are in a time-limited class, do not promote the game as a competition between teams. Do not recognize the 'fastest team'; instead have a reflective or writing activity for teams that have finished so that those students aren't sitting around with nothing to do. In the sample game, we do this by having a time-focused activity at first, which leads into a role-playing activity and then a reflective activity where the time limit is no longer a part of the narrative.

The second lesson is to *select appropriate learning outcomes* for the escape game. Escape game challenges are not ideal for every learning outcome. If players are required to explore, to create, or to think deeply about something, that will not be successful in a time-based game. Role-playing challenges don't work well under time pressure, as players just want to find the phrase or ask the question that will let them 'unlock' the gate to continue with the game.

There are two types of learning outcomes that work well in a time-focused game. The first is when you are using the game to introduce a concept to the students as the initial activity in a section of content for a class. The escape game could be used to help the students understand the real-world situation where a class topic is important, for example, by playing a time-focused simulation. Even under time pressure, players will get the brief exposure and hopefully gain interest in learning more about the topic as they see the value of learning it. Another type of learning outcome that works well is an assessment-based outcome, where the game is designed to help players know if they have mastered a topic. This is especially true if the players will need to perform on a timed exam, and the puzzles in the room map to the same processes the players need to succeed in the timed exam. In this case, the goal of the game is not learning about the topic, but instead seeing if you have learned about the topic, so the time-focused gameplay is less of an issue.

The third lesson is to *focus on the post-game reflection*. In Chapter 8, we will explore how to facilitate a reflective activity in the game. It is during this reflection where the players can think about what they have done to achieve the goals, and have those reflective moments to reach learning outcomes that require mental processing and deep thought. A good rule of thumb is to reserve one-third of the class time for reflection about the activity, or to build those reflective activities into the game, as we have done in the sample game. If you know the types of reflective questions you want the players to answer up front, then you can design challenges with the hooks that you will use for the reflections. A good learning game experience comes from the post-game reflection more than the game itself.

Eliminate Tangible Rewards

Because classrooms are reward-focused environments, it is a natural inclination for teachers to want to provide students with an incentive for completing the game. This might be recognition for finishing the game faster than everyone else, or candy placed in the final box, or affiliating a grade with the completion of the game in time. Just as with time limits, these tangible rewards have the same impact – they encourage the players to focus on doing only what needs to be done to figure out the code for the locks instead of engaging fully with the challenge. Many recreational puzzle hunts offer rewards for the teams that finish the fastest, and because of this the winning strategy for puzzle hunters focuses on finding the answer above all else. People new to puzzle hunts who enjoy doing puzzles will quickly find that when paired with players who want to win, they will be frustrated, as they will be discouraged to work on a puzzle that someone has already cracked the answer code for. An example would be a jigsaw puzzle, where the players are looking to figure out a message from the puzzle; players focused on the tangible reward will only do enough of the puzzle to get the message, and then sweep that away to focus on the next challenge. If the learning outcomes are reached not by finding the message, but by doing the puzzle, then the players will not reach those outcomes if they are hyper-focused on getting a tangible reward.

Another problem with using tangible rewards is that it sends a message. Grades and rewards send the message that the activity will not be engaging and they need an incentive to participate. As Alfie Kohn says in his book *Punished by Rewards*, any presentation of 'if you do this, then you get that' implies that the 'that' is better than the 'this'. 'If you eat your vegetables, then you get your dessert' implies that the vegetables are the unpleasant thing, and the dessert is the pleasant thing (Kohn, 1993). If you present your escape game with an incentive for completing the game, you are sending the same message to the players – that the game is not going to be an enjoyable activity in its own right, but is a task you must perform for the reward.

If your game requires a reward to get people to play it, it's not a good game. The gameplay itself is the reward. This is one of the problems with the 'worksheets and locks' design concept at the heart of many breakout boxes – the activities are not engaging, so need the incentive to get people to play. The escape game itself should be presented as the reward, not the requirement to get the reward. Your game is the dessert, not the vegetables! If you use a tangible reward once, then the learner's expectations will be set for future escape games, and they will become goal-focused instead of process-focused, so don't start down this path of incentivizing play.

THE THEORY OF FLOW

One of the core philosophies in game design is the theory of flow, created by Mihály Csíkszentmihályi (1990). The basic concept of 'flow' when applied to game design is that the game should start out easy, and as the player gets better, the game should get more challenging. If the game is too hard at the beginning, then it can be frustrating for the players. If the game doesn't get more difficult, then the game can be boring. Applying this concept to escape game design means that the challenges should get more difficult as the game continues.

In this application, flow is very similar to the educational theory of Vygotsky's (1978) 'zone of proximal development' (ZPD). In this theory, the concept starts with the learner trying to reach a learning outcome, but there is a large gap between the learner and the outcome. It is the job of the educator to create a scaffold that will allow the learner to move to the outcome. Each layer of the scaffold connects to the ZPD, which is the space where the learner could reach with assistance. Once the learner moves toward the learning outcome, the zone moves with the learner, and the scaffolding can then change to help the learner move forward. Using the design concept of flow helps to create that scaffolding to take the learner from what they already know to reaching the learning outcomes.

Putting these concepts together creates a model for the design of an escape game (see Figure 7.3). At the start, the initial narrative, environment, and challenges should be designed around where the learners are in relation to the learning outcomes. Then, the escape game activities act as a scaffold that help the learners move toward the learning outcomes. The teacher can play a role in ensuring that the learners are understanding what they are doing, so that the game can be effective in bringing about the learning outcomes.

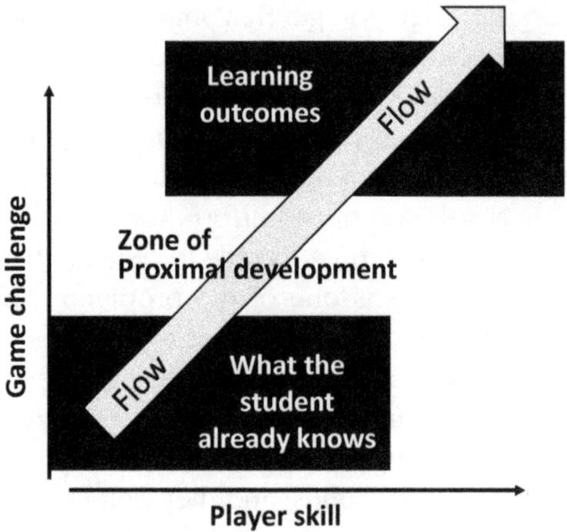

Figure 7.3 Combining the models for flow and ZPD

'DEATH BY THE BOOK'

In 'Death by the Book', an escape game to revise bookkeeping skills, one of the directors of a packaging company has been found dead, and foul play is suspected. The players are called in because the company's own accountant has fallen under suspicion, so the students take on the role of auditors investigating the accounts of the company to see if they can reveal a motive for murder. The emails, messages, and notes from the police inspector and the coroner ask questions about the crime that can only be answered by recalling and using the appropriate formulas to complete various elements of the company's accounts. In the exam, the students will be asked to put together a set of accounts, and to compare two sets of accounts, so the game was designed to test these skills.

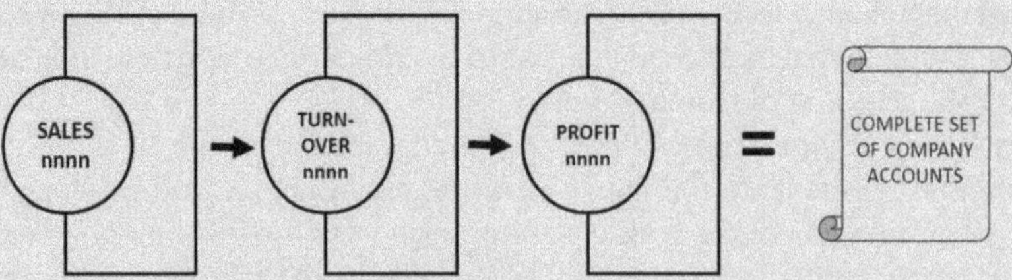

Figure 7.4 Game flow for 'Death by the Book'

There were nine puzzles, the answers to which were key numbers in the profit and loss statement, or the sales ledger, or other real-world document types, and then used as the codes for the padlocks. The game was presented using the linear model, as future calculations relied on the previous answers being right. This format also ensured that the whole group worked together through the process at the same time, with the more capable students leading the others.

The puzzles all had a very similar format, led by the narrative: two pieces of information that the players had to find and combine with the correct process to get the answer. Sometimes these formats are called 'story puzzles' or 'story problems' as they rely on the players comprehending what it is they are being asked to do, and applying the right formula.

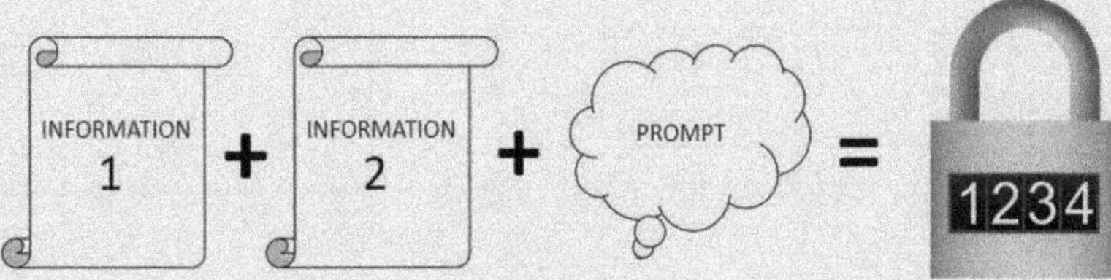

Figure 7.5 Puzzle format for 'Death by the Book'

To make the puzzles more challenging as the game went on, additional layers were added. For example, the players were given piles of receipts (lots of paperwork = teamwork!) and had to realize that as they only needed to use the receipts for the current accounting year, they needed to eliminate several receipts from the pile that had the wrong date on them. They also needed to know that the dates of an accounting year are not the same as a calendar year and know where to find that information. Yet another layer was added by having a couple of receipts undated, so the players had to cross-reference these purchases with other crime scene evidence to rule them in or out of that year's accounts. This example demonstrated the theory of flow, as the challenges all got more complex as the game went on, which helped the players feel engaged throughout.

USING THE THREE-ACT STRUCTURE TO SUPPORT FLOW

Earlier in the book, we explored developing a narrative using a three-act structure. In the puzzle design chapters, we talked about using the challenges to convey the narrative. During Act I, the players are being introduced to the world and the characters within that world. The challenges can be designed to help immerse the players in the world by having the components for the challenge be things that are unique to that setting, or by having them solve the challenge by doing actions that make sense in that world. During Act II, the challenges should become more intense and focus on the primary challenge of the game. Act II should end with the greatest challenge put forth by the opposition, which might be something that requires multiple attempts, so that the players fail, learn, and try again. Using a gate to trigger 'the twist' in the story is effective during Act II. From a learning perspective, Act III is the time for reflective activities. The players see the impact of what they have done. Rather than being a win–lose puzzle, Act III is a good time for a creative activity, such as responding to questions from a reporter or coming up with an impromptu speech about what happened. Building these reflective activities into the game will help add context to the learning outcomes and make it more likely that the game will have a long-lasting effect.

REFERENCES

Csikszentmihályi, M. (1990) *Flow: The Psychology of Optimal Experience*. New York: Harper and Row.

Kohn, A. (1993) *Punished by Rewards: The Trouble with Gold Stars, Incentive Plans, A's, Praise, and Other Bribes*. Boston: Houghton Mifflin Co.

Vygotsky, L.S. (1978) *Mind in Society: The Development of Higher Psychological Processes*. Cambridge, MA: Harvard University Press.

8 PROTOTYPING AND PLAYTESTING

A critical step in any game development process is prototyping and playtesting the game. This is an invisible step to the eventual players, but if it is not done, chances are high that there will be significant problems in the game. Many first-time game designers go straight into creating their 'final' version of a game after designing the concepts, and are then disappointed when they have people play the game and realize they have made decisions that make it unplayable.

Prototyping and playtesting is a cyclical process. After designing the ideas and developing the challenges, the next step is to make a testable prototype. Then, playtesters work through that prototype, and the designer returns back to the design process to deal with the problems that came up during testing. The designer creates another version of the game, has people playtest it, and then revises it again. Because of this process, it is best to use as few resources as possible in creating these early prototypes, as they will most likely be changed after one play.

As this cycle repeats, the scope of the changes usually gets smaller, so the designer can create more refined prototypes. At this stage, it is useful to create prototypes that are closer to the final version, so that the designer can test aspects of the physical build. After multiple successful playtests where nothing is changed, the designer can then create their final version of the game. It is important to playtest the final version in order to catch any mistakes made in creating this version.

BUILDING THE PAPER PROTOTYPE

Your first goal is to create a 'minimum viable prototype', which is as little as possible and will allow you to explore the challenges. The game can be mocked up on paper with descriptive text and/or diagrams instead of physical props. The goal at this point is not to replicate the experience of the game, but rather to see if the challenges are well designed and reach the learning outcomes. This is also not the time to worry about final art and graphics. Some graphics will need to be created if they are part of the challenge, but line art, placeholder images, and clip art are fine to use when possible.

Paper prototypes can be used not only for challenges that will be in the physical world, but also challenges that will be in the digital world. The facilitator can take on the role of 'the computer', and can have printed versions of what the player will see on the screen. As the player interacts with the paper prototype of the digital content, the facilitator can then move the paper around in response to simulate the computer program.

Physical elements of the game should also be created out of paper when possible. If paper is too thin, then cardstock can be used for these early prototypes. As with other types of puzzles, the goal at this stage is to invest as little as possible into the physical construction until the game has been playtested. A piece of paper with a padlock showing the type of lock can substitute for a real lock, and an envelope can substitute for a box.

If the plan is to use elements in a room as part of the game, that can be tested with paper. Basic room layouts can be drawn, showing key elements (and other elements that will be in the room decor), and players can point to what they want to explore during a playtest. To test the physical layout of props, index cards with the names of specific items or pictures of items can be printed out and put around the room.

EARLY PLAYTESTS

Instead of developing the entire game before having anyone play it, it is better to have someone playtest each challenge as it is created. This will help you better understand how difficult a challenge is to a player before you spend the time developing the entire game. You will want to eventually playtest the entire game with new playtesters, but at first, it's better to test one challenge at a time.

The first playtests of your game will probably not go very well. As Scott likes to warn first-time puzzle designers: 'Your game is too hard.' You've spent considerable time thinking about the learning outcomes, the world, the settings, and designed and revised your puzzles, but your players are brand new to all of it. There will be things that you now take for granted about your game design that your playtesters will not know, and this will likely be the source of your first problems with your game. You should have an idea of how long your puzzle should take, and most likely it will take much longer than that the first time through. This is normal.

If your puzzles are too hard, it could be due to one of several issues (assuming that there are no mistakes in the instructions or the puzzle). A common problem is that the puzzle requires the players to make too large of a mental leap (an 'a-ha') from what they currently know to what they need to know to be able to work on the puzzle. To solve this problem, you need to add more touchpoints that help move the users from where they are to where they need to be: more detailed instructions, a sample puzzle that is already solved, a partial solution for the puzzle, or guidance to help the player solve the first stage of the puzzle. Another way to solve the problem is to provide partial feedback to the user when they are correct or incorrect; if the feedback is only provided when a puzzle is completely solved, the players may not be confident that their actions are correct and continue to try different approaches to the puzzle.

As you add these tools to make the puzzle easier, there may be a point where the puzzle becomes too easy. This may not be a problem if the act of solving the easy puzzle still brings about the learning outcome, as this will then provide more time to add a reflective activity to anchor the learning. Adding more steps to a puzzle when those additional steps do not move the players toward a learning outcome is not recommended, as that makes the puzzle more tedious without benefit. Instead, it is better to add an additional layer to the puzzle, where the players will then use the results from reaching the goal state in a different way to further explore the learning outcomes or narrative.

CONTINUING THE DEVELOPMENT PROCESS

After going through several rounds of playtesting and revising, you should find that there are fewer changes needed after each test. Once the game design stabilizes, you can create prototypes that are closer to the final product. Paper can be laminated for use with dry-erase markers, so that new versions don't have to be printed out between each test. As students are used to writing on paper, any paper items in a game might be written on by an enthusiastic player. Games can be ruined for players because a previous group wrote notes in the margins of a book or other paper item.

Cardboard and foam core are useful at this stage to create game elements and puzzles that are more robust. Cardboard and duct tape are inexpensive and easy tools to create a prototype that can be used for multiple playtests without recreating it each time. To create a more long-lasting version, use foam core that is glued together and then painted with a non-water-based paint or varnish.

Another shortcut during this development time is to repurpose other things. A cardboard box with a hole punched near the edge in both the lid and the base can hold a padlock; if the cardboard starts to tear, then reinforce it with tape. Many plastic toolboxes have an eye for inserting a lock, and it is easy to add a hasp to an old wooden box to be able to attach a lock. Any bag from a zippered pouch to a suitcase with two zippers can hold a lock as well. Cable ties can loop through holes in anything to create a rudimentary closure that takes a padlock.

The goal at this point in the process is to test a prototype version of the game that is robust and close enough to the desired final product enough times, until you are comfortable there won't be additional changes. As a side note, there will always be additional changes; it is amazing what will slip through every round of testing and review, and not pop up until the day of the game.

The next level in creating game props that will last for many plays is to create them out of wood, metal, or plastic. Of these, wood is the easiest to work with and is also easy to repair, but is also more susceptible to damage. If you are spending the time to create a wooden prop, ensure it is sanded to protect the players from splinters and either varnished or painted to help the wood last longer. Metal is harder to work with (and can be dangerous if sharp edges or burrs are left), but will create extremely durable props. An advantage of plastic is by using a 3D printer or silicon molds and acrylic, it can be easy to create many identical copies (and backups) of the same item.

For many escape room puzzles, a laser cutter may be a better tool than a 3D printer. The laser cutter is excellent at cutting shapes out of wood and acrylic, and can also etch information on top of the shapes. Laser cutters are much faster than 3D printers, and as there are fewer settings they are usually easier to use to find the settings that will be successful. Vinyl cutters can then be used to cut out shapes like letters and symbols to attach to the surface.

If you don't have the time or resources to create items, you can buy blanks of pretty much anything – pill bottles, test tubes, wooden blocks and boxes, even blood bags (!) – and these can then be brought into the storyworld with labels, signs, branding, and decoration. Tea staining followed by a layer of PVA matte varnish is a great way of both aging and fortifying paper props. Craft and hobby stores are great for inspiration, but the best prices are online. If you are buying for multiple copies of a tabletop game, use 'wholesale' in your search term. Finally, it can be useful to ask someone who works in the industry that uses those items for real-world purposes; something that is hard to get on the market may be sitting in a junk heap somewhere, ready to be repurposed.

CHANGING THE SCALE

When creating tasks for educational puzzle-based games, think about the scale of the props needed for each puzzle and the number of elements needed to make the puzzle big enough to involve as many of the team members as possible. If you have teams of five, then design puzzles that scale to that number. Don't have one sheet of paper to decode, but five sheets that have to be decoded and then put together. Or you could make a puzzle that is very large – so all the players can work on it together, or at least see it so that they can shout out instructions and suggestions.

You can also create large-scale tasks where the players are using their full body to engage in the task. Searching a space can be seen as a large-scale task, as the players have to physically move around the venue. If there are elements of the narrative or the world that are built into the space (using environmental storytelling), then having large-scale tasks will require players to engage and familiarize themselves with the environment, and the storyworld it is part of.

In one game set on a building site, we used six-foot guttering pipes with different stripes on each for a puzzle. When the pipes were stacked on top of each other in the right order to create a rectangle, a pattern was revealed. In another game set in a nursery, we used the same puzzle made out of pick-up sticks. In a library-based game, we used the same idea on the spines of books that the students had to discover from partial clues in a booklist. This time, they had to be stacked by order of Dewey numbers to get the reveal. All of these are the same puzzle layer, but for different learning outcomes and at different scales.

THE PROCESS OF PLAYTESTING

There are risks to not getting a puzzle right. When your players come up with an entirely valid solution for a valid reason, supported by materials in your game, and it doesn't work, they feel cheated. They disengage from the game and from the learning opportunity it provides. Their memory of this learning experience becomes one of being tricked or short changed, and they lose trust in you. This is not the attitude you want to create in them towards learning, or towards you as their teacher. It is important to ensure every puzzle is fit for purpose. The task of making puzzles involves much throwing away of ideas that don't work, or mothballing them until you find inspiration about how to make them fit.

A puzzle is not a well-designed puzzle if:

- There are multiple solutions.
- You can guess the solution from only some of the information.
- The solution is written down somewhere for the players to find.
- You only have to complete part of the puzzle to get to the solution. For example, this piece with the magnet on it is the only one they *need* to put in the correct position and it opens the lock; the others pieces they can put anywhere, we'll just make it look like they are needed.
- The players have to guess some or all of the digits of the solution.
- The players have to guess some or all of the order of the solution.
- It is a red herring – that is, a complete puzzle that is a deliberate diversion.

You can't entirely trust that games or puzzles that you download obey these rules, even if you have bought them. Even games run by other teachers and subsequently sold online often have poorly designed puzzles. It has happened that we've even downloaded games that have wrong answers based on the information given, even when multiple reviews are resoundingly positive.

The more mainstream that escape rooms become, and the more often students are exposed to escape games in the classroom, the more they will be played by savvy and critical students, and so any poorly thought-out games will be exposed for what they are. You can mitigate against this somewhat by enrolling students in the process of playtesting the game – even though they may be playing the game in full and in earnest. It gives them a neutral topic to discuss, allows you as the teacher to model receiving and responding to feedback, and you could kill two birds with one stone by having one group critique and co-design a game aimed at another group entirely, for different levels of learning outcomes.

Briefing the students beforehand that they are going to be playtesting and feeding back on the game also removes some of the pressure students feel to achieve. There is often one in a group who will announce 'I hate this kind of thing', or 'I'm no good at this', or 'I can't do this'. If the students believe it's a valid response to say the puzzle is too hard, or takes too long, or doesn't work, that releases them from the worry that they might fail in the moment.

You might want to start the games by saying, 'I'd really appreciate your feedback at the end', and then depending on how the game goes, can make this a bigger or smaller part of the debrief. You can ask questions of your players such as:

- What learning points do you think the game designer was trying to get across?
- Did the challenges work to bring about the learning?
- How would you design a puzzle to get that across?
- How much did you follow the narrative and care about the outcomes?
- How would you make it better?

Player briefing is important – let them know what the boundaries are of the game and your solutions. Let them know you have never just written down an answer for them to use, otherwise they will try every number you have in the game as a solution, from the date on a newspaper clipping to the time the clock happens to be showing when they glance at it.

It is important to go into the playtest with an open mind. It can be frustrating to watch players struggle with something that you think is obvious, but if tester after tester does not solve the challenge, then something needs to be changed. This is also why multiple play-tests are important; something that one person doesn't understand may work out for the next three playtests. A challenge with playtesting puzzles is that once someone has tried a puzzle, they now have too much information to try it again and give you a fair playtest.

You need to test every puzzle you have designed in isolation, so you can get an idea of the time it takes to solve, and what distracts the players or detracts from their experience. Sometimes even the position you put the elements in relation to each other to start with can unconsciously bias the players to solving a puzzle a certain way. If you are finding that people need hints for one layer of your puzzle, then add a hint or nudge to help people succeed; players should not have to ask the facilitator for a hint to succeed at the game.

PLAYTESTING AND A PIGPEN CIPHER

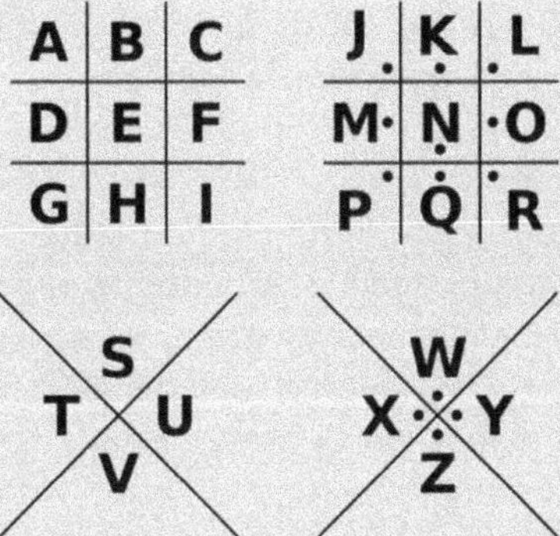

Figure 8.1 Pigpen cipher

We used a pigpen cipher as a starter puzzle for a game, which revealed the codes to open a briefcase. This cipher is unusual in that all of the symbols have rotational symmetry with other symbols, so we created the cipher to fit a square grid, which could be read starting from any corner, but only one version makes sense. Having the puzzle with four different viable angles to test solutions means that four players can be involved in solving the puzzle at once. When we playtested, we had the code grid blue-tacked squarely to the top of the briefcase, but at 90 degrees to how it would be read in that position. The briefcase was then placed flat on a table with the code grid facing upwards. We expected the players to turn the code around, or turn the briefcase around, and realize those affordances of being able to be read from any one of four angles. However, nine times out of ten the players simply didn't try this. We noticed they also weren't moving the briefcase at all; they were acting as though it was stuck in place, even when it wasn't.

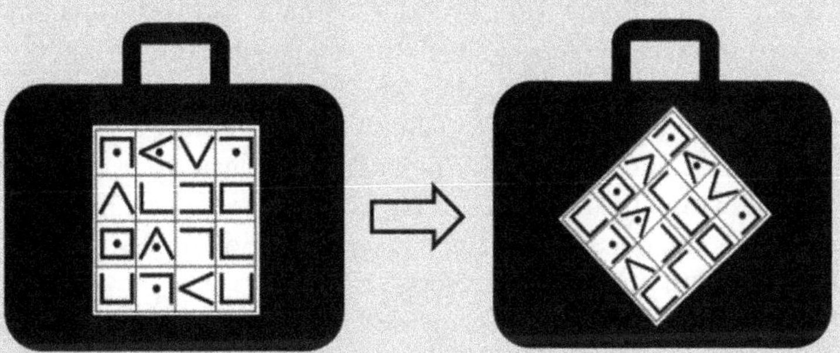

Figure 8.2 Briefcase with pigpen cipher puzzle

(continued)

To resolve this, we stuck the cipher grid onto the briefcase at a 45-degree angle, and had the players find the briefcase standing upright, so the first thing they had to do was pick the case up and put it down at whatever orientation they chose. Immediately, this made the players start questioning which way was the right way round, and begin by solving that layer of the puzzle.

If searching for the puzzle components is designed as part of the puzzle, you will need to playtest this too. If you hide things too well, your players will get frustrated and waste precious learning time. Even putting something on the bottom of the locked box they have to open is missed so often because of the unconscious bias of leaving the box how it was found in case that in itself is a clue.

Make a note of questions you want to ask your players before you start the playtest, and if they can wait until the end, don't be tempted to jump in whilst the playtest is still happening. Ask your playtesters to talk you through their thought process out loud if you can. This can even be done testing a digital game with the players recording themselves or simply noting down their thoughts as they approach solving the puzzle, or by sharing their screens and audio as they work through the challenge. If you are going to be in the same room as the playtesters, watching them, you need to gain a poker face. Even a glance or a raised eyebrow may be read or misread as a clue by the players.

A good rule of thumb is to ensure that a stage of a puzzle should take no longer than five minutes to solve once the players know what to do. After five minutes, the puzzle is probably too complex for a short escape game, and needs to be simplified or broken down into smaller tasks or stages. Sometimes the task at the heart of the puzzle, if it involves all the team members, may take a little longer as this is, after all, the learning objective you are aiming to meet.

Once you have tried out every puzzle individually, you need to find out what happens when players are faced with elements of several puzzles at once. You may already have decided the gating and flow of the game, and so you can test whether you have got this right. Players put the oddest things together sometimes, and you may find that two puzzles that worked well on their own suddenly interfere with each other in unexpected ways. This may mean redesigning one or more of the puzzle elements, so the connection that the players are making is removed, or putting the entire contents of one puzzle and all its components behind a gate later in the game, so that it doesn't interfere with an earlier puzzle. Try not to have more than one of each type of padlock visible at any one time, so if the players have discovered a code, they know which padlock they can open with the code.

When playtesting the locked room game described in Chapter 2, it became apparent that no matter where the teams started, and what order they did the puzzles in, the first table was the most difficult as they were getting used to the format and the padlocks, as well as solving puzzles. In addition, the teams always got faster as they went along, independent of which order they solved the tables in. Therefore, the final game doesn't allow 15 minutes per round; instead, it starts with a 20-minute round, then two 15-minute rounds, and then the final round in the remaining time.

ADDING THE SOCIAL ELEMENT

As escape games are more than just a series of puzzles, there may be moments where the players interact with someone from the storyworld. This can all be done through written or recorded media, such as by reading a series of letters or emails, or through a diary that leads the players through the challenges. Reading a long text during a game is typically not very successful, as either one player reads it and only shares what is critical, or one player quickly reads it out loud while everyone else ignores it whilst working on other puzzles. Having an interaction with a person can be more impactful, especially if it is done in small amounts.

When you are playtesting the puzzles, you will also be playing the role of any non-player characters the players may meet. This may also be how it is run for the game, but when one teacher is trying to handle ten student groups, it can be challenging to interact with each group. In addition, if there are critical elements that need to be passed along to the players, a human playing the role live adds the risk of forgetting to say something. Recordings can alleviate a number of these problems. These recordings could be video, but many times an audio recording is just as useful while being much easier to produce and share.

Recording character interactions ahead of time has some advantages and disadvantages. It ensures that everything that needs to be said is shared every time in a consistent way. Using talking head video also allows the injection of photographs or video clips to provide more information. If the players are in control of the recording, they can listen to it multiple times to ensure everyone knows what is going on. The main disadvantage is that the players can't ask questions for clarification; that said, in many cases, in a live interaction, this type of clarification can end up adding red herrings to the challenge.

If you are going to have a live interaction with players, it will be important to document what should be said. During the early playtests, the interactions will be improvised, but as you playtest and learn what the players need to know, the scripted elements can be developed. It is useful to create a list of those pieces of information that must be shared with the team, information that might be useful for the players if they ask the right questions, and extra details that aren't needed to overcome the challenges, but allow the interactions to be consistent with the world.

One way to ensure that the players take away what was important after a social interaction is to write up 'notes' that the players get after the encounter with the non-player character. Giving the teams notes after the discussion reduces the chance of confusion, as it helps the players to know what was important and to make sure they have the details correct.

PREPARING FOR THE ESCAPE GAME EVENT

One of the most important tools to develop at this point to prepare for the live event are checklists. Assuming that there will be multiple teams playing the game, then each team needs to have an identical copy of the game components. Therefore, having a checklist for what each team needs in their kit is essential. Another useful checklist contains the items that you have in addition to the individual team kits with things like backup puzzle components and tools to repair game elements on the spot, such as instant-set glue, duct tape, a small toolkit, scissors, and extra paper and cardstock.

Another useful checklist for the event is one that walks you through the room setup process. The day of the event can be nerve racking, and having a list to work through will increase the chances that everything will be in place. If the game is going to be run multiple times, then you need a reset checklist that takes you through, step-by-step, how to get the game from its end state back to its start state. If you run the same games regularly, you will internalize these checklists, but if the game is a one-off or run once a year, a written record is needed. It can be incredibly frustrating to have a team work through the challenges, open the final box, and find it is empty because you forgot to reset what goes in the box from the last time the game was played.

It can also be useful to have a schedule of activities with timing. If it is important that all of the teams reach a point in the story at a similar time, then you will need to know where they should be on earlier challenges to keep up with that pace. In the sample game, we have provided a game master's checklist with answers to each puzzle and brief notes on how each is solved, so that it can be quickly found during the game when helping frustrated teams. Writing hints ahead of time that are released on a schedule can help to ensure that all the teams are at a similar point in the game. Avoid the temptation to cut out the reflection time in order to give the players more time to work on the puzzles; it is better from a learning perspective to have done fewer things and have time to reflect than to do more things but with no time for reflection.

While running the game, it is important to monitor the progress of the teams. If teams are struggling, it might be because they haven't found a critical component needed to solve the puzzle … and that component is nowhere to be found. Your intervention can be the difference between a very frustrating session and a session where a mistake you made is quickly overlooked. In today's gaming world, 'patches' are very common as the tool for a game designer to fix a mistake in the game; making a joke about 'downloading a patch' while delivering a missing piece will help the players to put the mistake in perspective. Accept that mistakes in game design will happen and focus on providing the players what they need to have an engaging experience instead of dwelling on what 'should have been'.

9
RUNNING THE GAME: FACILITATION, REFLECTION, AND ASSESSMENT

In this final chapter before our sample game in Chapter 10, we will explore some of the key issues to consider when running the game. Escape games are not passive activities; commercial escape rooms pay a staff member to monitor players while they are playing, and you need to plan on playing an active role in the game as well. There are several important roles that you can play beyond the initial quest giver to ensure your players get the most out of the experience: you can monitor the players as you facilitate the game and provide hints, you can guide the players through a self-reflection that is critical in achieving learning outcomes, and you can help learners use these escape games as a formative assessment tool.

THE ROLE OF THE FACILITATOR

Consider the role of the facilitator in your escape game. There are a few models to follow:

- The facilitator is like a Game Master in a tabletop role-playing game. They are not part of the game, but an invisible helping hand. They may present the opening as a narrator, unless you have created media for that, and then will monitor the teams as they progress.
- The facilitator is a remote Ally. They are part of the game, but for some reason they can't be in the game space with the players. They will start off the game as a Game Master, but then shift into the Ally role. They will be on call for the players but may not be playing an active role. They will play more of an 'invisible hand' role in helping players, but in a way that maintains immersion. In the sample game, the Security Guard is a remote Ally. You can also play several remote allies in one game.
- The facilitator is an in-person Ally. In the storyworld, they are in the same space as the players. They can take a more active role in helping the players figure things out. There needs to be a story reason why they can't just solve the problems easily; this is usually accomplished by having the expertise of the Ally be in an area that is different than what is needed for the game, or they can be incapacitated by drugs, injury or illness.

There are other approaches as well – the player could be a Henchman (that might become an Ally), or the player could be the meddling Big Bad Guy who is there to watch them struggle with the challenges and provide droplets of information to ensure they continue. No matter the role, the facilitator's main job is to ensure the players are moving forward through the game.

This concept of keeping the players moving through challenges is important in an escape game for learning, as the challenges have been developed to reach specific learning outcomes. If the players get stuck on a challenge for a long time and do not have time to engage with all of the challenges, then they may not engage with all of the learning outcomes. It is better for the players to engage partially with each challenge than to struggle with one for too long (and beyond the point where it is helping them learn).

Watching for this point in the game – when the players are no longer going to learn from the struggle – is the most important role for the facilitator during the gameplay session. If players are not engaging with the challenge in a way that will benefit them, because they haven't figured out what the challenge actually is, then the facilitator needs to step in and get them going. If they have engaged with the challenge correctly, but can't figure it out, the facilitator has to decide if they have met the learning outcomes or not, and give hints as appropriate. Depending upon the situation, the facilitator may even provide the answer or manually move them on to the next challenge.

Depending on the shape of the game, either the whole class will accomplish the mission together, or only some of the teams will succeed. You need to decide on your hint policy and mechanism so that they support your learning objectives. In a game that is about social and collaborative skills being run as a group-builder, failure will give them as much to talk about as group success. However, if you are wanting the students to practice certain skills or cognitive strategies, enough hints, cues, and clues should be given that the mission will be a success – if the narrative is one where 'success' is achievable. The role of the facilitator is to ensure that the learning happens, and this means that if the students are paying attention and engaging with the game, they should be given every opportunity to win.

Dropping hints as the facilitator is a bit of a learned skill, but it is not so different from what teachers do every day. Create a hint script with timings for each game you design, and be prepared to playtest the hints too. Some commercial venues like to give cryptic hints, but in a classroom setting getting the students to ask each other or the teacher for help is one of the behaviors you want to encourage, so straightforward hints are better. Also, as your game is probably going to be linear, in order that all students have the whole experience, there is nothing else they can do once they have decided they are stuck and need a hint, so be as responsive as possible.

Hints should be given of increasing strength. A little nudge to start with might just get them looking at all the right elements of the next puzzle, so your job is to nudge the players away from what is irrelevant at that moment, and towards what they need for the puzzle in hand. Observing out loud can simply direct the players to the right track. Try to stay in character and respond as your character would, and instead of solving things, just draw their attention to the right place. If you find one of the players had a good idea that was ignored, you can ask them to repeat it or explain it for you, to get the rest of the players listening to them. If there is a tool needed such as a calculator for the next puzzle, draw the players' attention to it.

It might be that the players end up genuinely stuck, and no matter what you say or direct them towards, frustration is beginning to set in. Being a bit more direct with 'Have you tried this?' or 'Does this have anything to do with it?' may give them the kickstart they need. If that doesn't work, use some of the pertinent keywords, including the names of equations, methods, or authors, and so on to get them to recall their relevant knowledge. You could prepare worked examples for some types of puzzles that you can introduce in-character and ask if they might be of use for the students to use as exemplars. This is still getting the students to do the work, even though you have effectively taken the 'puzzle' out of it.

The act of noticing and paying attention to individual students is very valuable in building their trust and confidence. Take this opportunity to challenge yourself as the facilitator to find something noteworthy about each of the students. Perhaps there is also an opportunity for you to praise a student who finds the usual classroom formats difficult to conform to.

Try to give feedback to the students who didn't end up opening a lock. They may feel less successful than their teammates because they never got that payback moment. The feedback will be given in front of their teammates, and this is an opportunity to perhaps change the words used to describe some of the members of the class, basing the feedback squarely on what you have observed and the effect it had on the success of the team. It is sometimes the more introverted and/or neuro-diverse students who come into their own in an activity based on puzzles, and it's a great opportunity to reframe their skillset and value, for them and their classmates.

It is acceptable to change the game while it is going on in order to improve gameplay and create better opportunities for learning. If you can see that a puzzle is failing, if something slipped through the testing, or you are not going to have enough time to have a reflection, it is better to step out of character and back into the teacher role, and explain to the students what is happening. It can be very confusing to try to change the game while staying in-character (unless you are playing a role for which that makes sense), so if there needs to be a stop to the game, call a stop to the game. If the game involves physical activity and safety may be an issue, it is important to establish a signal (such as a whistle) that indicates all gameplay should stop immediately for safety concerns. One suggested safety note is to let all players know that if they are concerned for their own or someone else's safety, they should shout 'Stop' and put their hands above their head in an X. This isn't such a concern if the game takes place seated at tables, but if people are quickly moving around a space, then safety needs to be considered.

REFLECTION

John Dewey, a learning theorist, wrote that education is the combination of experience and reflection (Dewey, 1916). Without reflection, experience alone does not teach. Many who use games to teach depend upon the game as a standalone activity to educate players. But the experience of playing is simply not enough. The most important part of the game can be the reflection about what went on during the game. This needs to be planned as part of the escape game activity, and we recommend that one-third of the entire session be dedicated to wrapping up and debriefing the game.

The overarching goal of debriefing after an educational escape game is to help the players consider their experiences and connect those experiences to things they already knew. By doing this, the learning outcomes become part of their new knowledge about the world. One of the reasons this is important with escape games is the time limit that drives these games. When a player has a tight time constraint, they become focused on what they need to do to succeed. They will take shortcuts and will do only what is needed to get that lock open before the clock runs out.

While the time pressure is part of what creates the intense engagement with these games, it can also be the culprit in preventing students from having a reflective experience. This reflection needs to take place outside of the time-based goal of the escape game so that the player can pause, think, and connect their experiences to their own reality.

While some reflection can take place after the game is over in the player's own mind, reflection is more powerful when it is done in a group. If a player is not able to make the connections between what they did and their own mental scaffold, then the reflection is not going to have a significant impact. By hearing what insights other players had around the same experience, it raises the chances that an individual will find the connections between what they knew before and what they just did. Each person has a different mental scaffold, and the goal of a group debriefing is to help more people make connections between their prior knowledge and the experience.

A useful model for reflection after an activity was developed by Thiagi, an expert in corporate training and debriefing (Thiagarajan, 2004), and the questions below are inspired by that model. Walking the learners through these questions helps them start by focusing on the experience, then connecting that experience to themselves and the real world:

- How do you feel right now? After racing against a clock, asking a question about emotions helps the players to move out of the flow-based focused gameplay state into a self-reflective state.
- What happened in the game? As different groups probably had different experiences in the game, this is a chance for people to talk about their experience and learn how other player's viewpoints of their experiences were different. If the game is non-linear, this is particularly important, as there will be some people who didn't see some of the challenges.
- What did you learn from the game? This is where you are asking the players to connect the game to their prior knowledge. Different people will have learned different things from the same experience. It is more powerful to allow the learner to say what they learned than it is for you to tell them what they should have learned. It also will allow you as a designer to see if something in the game isn't doing a good job of reaching a learning outcome.
- How does this relate to the real world? While our suggestion is that the challenges in the game should be inspired by the real world, the players will see connections between what they learned and the real world that you never considered. Again, these connections are more powerful when they are presented by the players, but you can also bring up connections at the end of this phase if the learners didn't connect the activities to the real-world learning outcomes.
- What do we do next? This phase can take different directions, based upon the learning outcomes. You can ask questions about how to improve the game design to convey the learning outcomes. While they have explored one path that you created, they now may have ideas of how the game could be designed differently. Or you could ask questions about what might happen next in the story, which can give you direction for another escape game in the series. You could also ask about who else could benefit from playing the game, which can get them thinking as a teacher using the game to benefit others. By getting their creative designer juices flowing, it deepens the connection and can set the stage for you to have an assignment that has students creating challenges and games of their own!

Integrating Reflection into the Game

In the sample game, the reflection process starts in the game, as the players are asked to come up with a statement about what happened in the game and what might happen next as part of the game. When the reflection starts as an in-game activity, it is then natural to continue the reflection with other questions. To do this requires a 'change of stage', meaning the players have to be taken out of their context as solvers-of-puzzles and into a context that gets them to reflect upon what went on. This could be done by giving them a reflective task, such as talking to a reporter, writing an article, or reporting what happened to a higher power. This can also be done by changing their role in the game to make them a reporter, a decision maker, or a historian 50 years in the future who is looking back. It is also important to remove the time constraint for this portion of the activity, as reflection under time pressure may not be as effective.

If the reflection starts in the game, then the facilitator can move through the rest of the reflection process, moving the players gently out of the game space and back into the real world, much like a pilot landing a plane gently, and before you know it, you are back at ground level. This gentle landing helps the players to connect their game activities to their real-world activities and is more effective than the recreational escape room approach of opening the final door and exiting into the lobby, blinking from the bright lights and trying to reconnect with the world around.

HOW TO PROVIDE FEEDBACK AFTER AN ESCAPE GAME

As the game master and teacher, you are uniquely positioned to observe the game being played and then feedback to the students on what you observed. It is a great opportunity to not only watch the students, but to observe them in several different situations, dealing with several different problems, in swift succession.

While you are watching the game, make notes, mental or otherwise, on what the players do to help or hinder the group, on how they express themselves, how they work with other team members, and how they solve problems and puzzles. Notice what contributions they made, and value everything. When the timer stops, those students who got swept along in the flow of the game may be feeling vulnerable after realizing they have been acting without artifice in a situation that was both deliberately manufactured and observed. It's crucial that they are held in unconditional positive regard throughout the debrief process as well as the game.

It is always better to let the students go through self-reflection before you start reflecting and assessing. It is much more powerful for them to have their own 'a-ha' moments about what they did; it is slightly less powerful if they have an 'a-ha' moment while learning what their peers did; it is much less powerful if you tell them what they should have realized. Only after working through their own reflection should you give feedback on their performance. Here are some suggestions for tactfully giving feedback in a group setting:

State What You Noticed

Simply let the student know what you saw. Sometimes they don't realize that they made a crucial contribution to the solution. You don't have to judge it, and if you need to provide feedback to a student about something that could be seen as negative, phrasing it with a simple 'I noticed that you …' works well. For example:

- 'I noticed that you collected and organized all those records as you went along, so as soon as you got the last record in place, it was easy for the others to see the pattern.'
- 'I noticed that you had difficulty with the lock and so you asked for help rather than struggle on.'
- 'I noticed that you appeared frustrated and sat back for a while, then when there was another puzzle to solve you got straight back in there.'
- 'I noticed that you two worked together on that puzzle and solved it collaboratively.'

Helping students understand the impact of their contribution, however small they may have thought it, helps them understand and value their skills and abilities, which in turn helps build self-confidence.

Encourage a Growth Mindset

Challenge their expectations of themselves. Many students lack belief in their own abilities. You may have heard 'I can't do this', or 'I'm no good at X type of puzzles' from students before, sometimes even before you have explained the task. Students sometimes seem to expect defeat even before they have tried. Take every statement as a challenge to feedback something positive about the experience to them afterwards. Look for the moment when they *do* contribute, when they *do* come up with an idea or a solution, and at the end of the game repeat back their statement with evidence to the contrary: 'You said you couldn't do wordy puzzles, but it was you who figured it out in the end. Maybe you are better at solving problems than you think you are?'.

To encourage a growth mindset, Carol Dweck (2008) advises us to teach students that they can 'grow their brains', and they can do this by focusing on the processes that lead to learning, including trying new strategies, and seeking input from others when stuck. In fact, an escape game could be used specifically for the purpose of encouraging a growth mindset as it makes an ideal lab for experimentation and collaboration.

Provide Feedback on Their Own Feedback

Often players will spend some time, sometimes a lot of time, on the wrong solution. They may have a very good idea, but perhaps be working with an incomplete set of components, so that their solution just doesn't fit. They may state that they feel stupid or turn on the person who came up with the wrong idea. One way to deflect this is to talk about the solution they came up with, why it was wrong, and what misled them, but also under what circumstances it could have been right. Then end by agreeing that it's a really good idea for a puzzle and thank them for their assistance in designing your next game.

During the game, the players may congratulate each other and comment on each other's ideas and performance in a very supportive and appreciative way, but those precious moments can get lost in the heat of the game. Bring them out in the debrief if you can – ask the students to repeat what they said or, if you need to, you can repeat what you heard. This public appreciation may be a new experience for some class members; it will help build camaraderie in the team and class, and provide material for further reflection.

USING AN ESCAPE GAME FOR ASSESSMENT

We have discussed that escape games can be used to inspire students and help them get interested in a topic, but they can also be used after other forms of teaching as an assessment tool. It cannot be stated firmly enough that escape games should not be used for 'stealth assessment', where the players do not know that they are being assessed during the game. This is especially true if the plan is to provide a grade for performance. Escape games are *games*, which are play-based activities. Telling students that they will be playing a game while planning to secretly assess their abilities will lose trust with your students and hurt your ability to use these types of games again.

In general, it is not a good idea to use an escape game as a summative assessment tool where performance is graded. Because the escape games are designed to help the players have a set of experiences and providing hints are part of the game, having this translate into a class grade based on performance is problematic. There is a similar issue in recreational escape rooms that have leaderboards for the fastest times. In rooms where the game master is allowed to give hints to the players, there will be bias introduced in the game based upon the responsiveness of the game master and the quality of the hints provided. It is recommended that you use a simulation model instead of an escape game model if your goal is to do summative assessment with these challenges.

That said, escape games can be quite valuable as a formative assessment tool where performance is not graded. You can still evaluate the performance as discussed in the previous session and provide feedback, but in formative assessment, the goal is to use the assessment to identify what to focus on. The structure of a playful exploration of a topic, followed by a self-reflection and an evaluation is ideal for formative assessment.

If the goal of using the escape game is for formative assessment, then the challenges need to be developed to provide those opportunities for assessment. There should be much less focus on layers and puzzles that aren't related to the learning outcomes, and a more direct application of the game concepts to the skills that are to be assessed. When possible, there should be opportunities in the game for each student to be 'in charge' of their team in working through a challenge; a student won't be able to assess their own abilities if all they do is watch others take on a challenge. This can be done by assigning roles to each student and having specific tasks in the game that are led by the student in a specific role.

It is a natural fit to use an escape game to assess how a team works together. In the commercial escape room world, a popular use of escape games is as a team-bonding activity. A key difference is that in these team experiences, there are already pre-formed teams and the game allows the players to explore and expand upon their relationships. In a classroom setting, the group of students coming together may have never worked as a team before, in which case it is important to build the game around the developmental stages of team growth to help the group of people to come together and succeed.

Escape games can also be useful in assessing soft skills such as communication and delegation, as these are key skills in working together. If the game is structured around open-ended challenges without defined solutions, then the game can assess creativity and out-of-the-box thinking. It can also be used to assess the use of engineering and scientific methods of hypothesizing, prototyping, testing, assessing, and then applying that knowledge in a new situation.

Learner-Developed Games as an Assessment Tool

While playing one of these can create an exciting hour of class time, having students create an escape game for the classroom can be the basis for a multi-week project that requires creativity, logical thinking, and storytelling while allowing the learners to deepen their understanding of a topic area. In many ways, creating a game about a topic area is similar to teaching about a topic area. The developer of a game for learning, just like someone preparing to teach a topic, must:

- Have a thorough understanding of the topic area, to ensure the content is accurate.
- Understand what the learners already know before starting the game.
- Decide upon the specific learning outcomes for the game.
- Create activities that connect the learners from where they are to the learning outcomes.

A key part of an escape game assignment is the selection of learning outcomes. If the learning outcomes are based around trivia-style facts, the resulting games will be trivia-style puzzles. While an escape game can be created out of crossword puzzles and putting famous names into locks, it isn't the best use of the resources and time required to create an escape game. If the learning outcomes are fact-based, there are other types of assessments and games that are more appropriate than an escape game.

The best learning outcomes for an escape game are process-based outcomes. As escape games can include simulations, having learning outcomes that tie into simulations can lead to a successful project. In addition, it can be difficult to assess understanding of a process through more traditional paper-based methods, so creating a simulation to explore the process can lead to a better assessment tool. Other outcomes that are suitable are those that lead into a narrative, where the exploration of a story can help learners build empathy, understand different perspectives, or understand how things changed over time. Setting appropriate learning outcomes is the first step in ensuring that students can be successful at creating escape games.

Different Structures for Escape Game Assignments

Providing structure is important in any assignment involving design. Without structure, students can get overwhelmed with an assignment to create something they've never done before. Creating an escape game requires both creative writing for the story and characters, and technical writing for documenting puzzles appropriately. Having to build a functioning puzzle requires hands-on arts and crafts skills, and testing and redeveloping a game requires an engineering mindset. Because of all of these elements, they can be fantastic assignment structures for student groups where different skills are needed for success. But having to create everything is a longer-term class assignment.

There are different structures that can be used for these assignments. Chapter 2 explored a variety of game shapes, and starting with one of these gives the students some structure for the assignment. No matter which game shape is used, there are ways to structure these assignments so they are not overwhelming. These different structures could also be used iteratively over the course of a month or semester so that students continue to develop and improve their games.

1. Develop an escape game pitch: the first step in creating a game is to create the 'pitch', which is an overview of the entire experience. This pitch can be developed in PowerPoint to create a 'pitch deck', which is the industry standard of a starting point for a game. This pitch should contain an overview of the story, the major story beats, and the concepts for the challenges that convey the story beat. These pitch decks are used to present a high-level overview of the game and allow for

feedback at this early state where it is still easy to make decisions. Starting with a pitch will help avoid one of the traps of escape game design – designing a puzzle first that doesn't really fit in the overall scope of the game.

2. Develop a single challenge: for this assignment, the students are assigned to create a single puzzle or challenge that fits into a larger narrative. This helps focus the challenge down to the core activity for the game. For a class-wide developed escape game, this can serve as the first step for an iterative design activity.
3. Develop an escape game as a class from individual challenges: this builds on the previous activity. The class as a whole develop story beats, and then students are assigned to one story beat and associated learning outcome. Each student creates a challenge (which can be assessed as an individual assignment), and then they are put into groups with others that made challenges for the same story beat. Each group is then tasked to develop a more refined challenge by first testing everyone's individually designed challenges, and then working together to create a new challenge. The resulting game can then be run as a class for parents or other classes.
4. Develop an escape game as a class from mini-games: for this model, the overarching concept is developed as a class and broken apart into different game spaces. For example, if the game is to be in a science lab, there could be the Professor's Office, the Laboratory, the Storage Room, and the Secret Lair (because there's always a Secret Lair). The class is then divided into groups, and each group develops the story beats and activities for each of the spaces in the final game. This works well for playtesting, as each group can test the games of the other groups. The resulting game can then be run for parents or other classes.
5. Develop an escape game as a group: this is best presented as an iterative long-term project, where each group goes through all of the steps. The group starts with a pitch to the class, which is evaluated. They then develop the spaces and puzzles for the game, and test it with other groups. The resulting games can then be run in a large open house for parents or other classes. A good rule of thumb is one challenge for each five minutes of time.

For any of these projects, it's important to emphasize that the focus of the project is on the concept, the puzzle, and the tie into the learning outcome. These challenges can be made of cardboard or foamcore, or could use Minecraft, Scratch, or Google Forms. While challenges could be made with Arduino or Raspberry Pi and RFID tags, introducing this type of technology tends to get students focused on using technology, even when it doesn't make sense to use technology. Therefore, unless the focus of the class is to work with electronics, it's not recommended to push students to develop their challenges beyond paper and cardboard. If there needs to be 'technology' to make a puzzle work, this can be the role of a student in the testing, where they are playing the role of the magnetic lock or RFID tag to simulate technology.

Assessing the Students' Games

It can be valuable to the students if they have a rubric showing how their games will be assessed. This can help them understand what to focus on. As with other projects with an artistic component, students can be lured away from focusing on the important elements of the projects, such as the integration of learning outcomes, and instead making them flashy or pretty. This is part of the reason we suggest a focus on paper and cardboard, in order to reduce this temptation.

One of the most difficult parts of making an escape game challenge is getting the difficulty right. The only way this can be learned is through playtesting, so it is important to build in some required playtesting times during class. While some students will have access to other playtesters outside of the class, some will not, but it is crucial to be able to test out puzzles with others. Having the students keep a design journal as part of the process can help them to become more reflective designers and can help you better assess the process they went through.

An important question to have students ask themselves is: 'What would someone know after doing your challenge that they did not know before?' This question – how does the game change a player? – needs to be at the heart of the design task. When making design decisions, the goal with each change is to make it something that does a better job of reaching the learning outcome. If faced with multiple paths to the learning outcome, then the designer can think about integration with story and narrative, and finally the concept of Leville's 'rounding up to fun' comes into play (Nicholson, 2016). By thinking about the learning outcomes throughout the design process, the students will end up also engaging with the learning outcomes in a more meaningful and deeper way than they would through other, less active, learning techniques. The games they create will serve as evidence for outcome-based assessment processes, and for students looking to head to university they can become part of their portfolio.

REFERENCES

Dewey, J. (1916) *Democracy and Education: An Introduction to the Philosophy of Education*, New York: Macmillan.

Dweck, C. (2008) *Mindset*. New York: Ballantine.

Nicholson, S. (2016) Ask Why: Creating a Better Player Experience Through Environmental Storytelling and Consistency in Escape Room Design. Paper presented at Meaningful Play 2016, Lansing, MI. Available online at http://scottnicholson.com/pubs/askwhy.pdf.

Thiagarajan, S. (2004) Six Phases of Debriefing: Play for Performance. Available online at http://thiagi.net/archive/www/pfp/IE4H/february2004.html#Debriefing

10
SAMPLE GAME: 'MISINFORMATION LITERACY'

To close out the book, here is a sample game that you can photocopy, cut out, prepare, and use in a classroom. The topic of the game is information literacy and is appropriate for different age groups in different ways.

For older students (14+), groups of four can work through the game on their own, and the game can be the inspiration for discussions and traditional class content. For students aged 10–14, this game would work well after more traditional lessons as a summary activity. For younger students, the game could be worked through as a class, with the instructor leading each of the challenges, and the class divided into small groups all working on the same task at the same time.

The game can be presented all in one sitting, where it would take about 45 minutes of playtime, which would leave 15 minutes to talk about the implications of the game. The game is designed in two independent halves, so it could also be played in two 30-minute sessions over different weeks.

There are four different ways to implement this game, based upon the amount of facilitation desired and the resources available.

Self-check:
No locks or facilitator needed. Players check their answers and open the next envelope when their answer matches a condition on the envelope. You will need two envelopes of different sizes to act as containers, as one will nest inside the other.

Facilitated:
The players bring their answers to a facilitator who gives them the next envelope when they have the correct code.

Padlocks:
The players work out a code to open each padlock to continue. You need two four-digit locks, one five-letter/number lock, and a multi-lock hasp, plus three lockable containers. It's preferable to have nested containers, so the players always know which type of lock they have to open next (and aren't tempted to fiddle with them), although you could also have the containers side by side.

Digital:
The entire game is available digitally at http://scottnicholson.com/misinformation. Note that there is a limited hint system in the digital version, so you will still need to be available to help people if they are struggling. You may want to go through this first to experience the game as a player before reading the rest of the game.

For any version except for the digital version, you will need to photocopy and cut apart everything in the Components section, and make one copy of the game for each team of three to four players. There are also posted Resources as printable PDFs on the website at http://scottnicholson.com/misinformation. If your plan is to use the materials again, then everything should be laminated, and the players supplied with a dry-erase marker. Know that if things are not laminated, players will make marks on the papers as they are solving the puzzles (even if you ask them not to). The computer screen should be created as a two-sided document with a front and back. Photocopy or print out these resources now, so you have them to hand as you read the rest of the document.

The game is presented in several parts. First is the overview, which will give you the flow of the game. Second is the in-depth challenge discussion, which talks through the details of the learning outcomes and how to set up each challenge. Third are the resources, which are the pages to photocopy to play the game and a checklist to guide you in assembling the game. There are some design notes at the end, to give you an insight into how to design the puzzles to help you with your own game designs.

Overview

The game is set in Liz's storyworld, which was introduced in Chapter 3. The players are tasked by the University of Northern England (UNE) to sneak into the research library located at the main offices for the biotech organization Mobius. They know that Mobius is planning a misinformation campaign, and their goal is to figure out what they are trying to do, why they are trying to do it, and to stop it if possible. The players are given a sheet of fake fingerprints, and their goal is to figure out which one to use to get deeper into Mobius. They have snuck to the library at Mobius during the lunch break, so they have to complete their mission and get out before the staff return in an hour.

They have a security guard (played by the facilitator) on the inside who can get them into the library and can watch for any trouble, but won't be of much use in finding what they need. UNE will be monitoring their progress and will provide sporadic updates and guidance through silent messages.

In the library, there are three challenges and a fingerprint scanner.

- The first is 'Spot the Bots', where the players must pick out the three bot accounts from printouts from a social media account and identify where they all come from.
- The second is 'Fake News', where the players compare three printouts of the same story from the same newspaper and look for clues as to which one is the fake fingerprint, whilst learning more about the Fingerprint Faker.
- The third is 'Graph Grifting', where the players read misleading graphs where the visualization of data doesn't reflect the real data, and where the players learn about Mobius employees. With the information from the three challenges, they can figure out which fake fingerprint to use on the scanner to enter a lab, or they can use the code from the fingerprint to open a four-digit padlock.

The players then enter the Data Center for Mobius. This is an office full of computers, and there is a screen on the largest computer displaying 'Hacking Attempt in Progress', with two choices: 'log on' or 'shut down', along with a password and authenticator data entry field. The players learn that the university has found an active internet forum of Hackers breaking into Mobius's system. Mid-transmission, this will be interrupted by the Hackers who are watching the video security feed, and who demand that the players log on to the system so they can continue their hack.

In 'Password Prying', the players will have to figure out the current password by examining the patterns of past changed passwords. They also need the PIN to unlock the authenticator field, which they can determine by piecing together still photographs of someone entering a passcode. Filling in the 'digital' display spaces that correspond to the password and PIN lead to the phrase CORRECT. They then have a choice – do they shut it down, or do they log on? They are interrupted with a role-playing activity, where they play out a radio interview between Mobius and the Hackers in order to help them understand the moral quandary. They then must choose to 'shut down' the system to protect it, or 'log in' to the system to allow access to the Hackers.

Either way, the university will reach out after this is complete and ask them to put together a 250-word news brief explaining what has happened, as a reporter has been alerted and is calling for a statement. This is the start of the reflection process, where the players then reflect upon the activities in the game in order to help them better understand the learning outcomes.

PRE-GAME BRIEFINGS

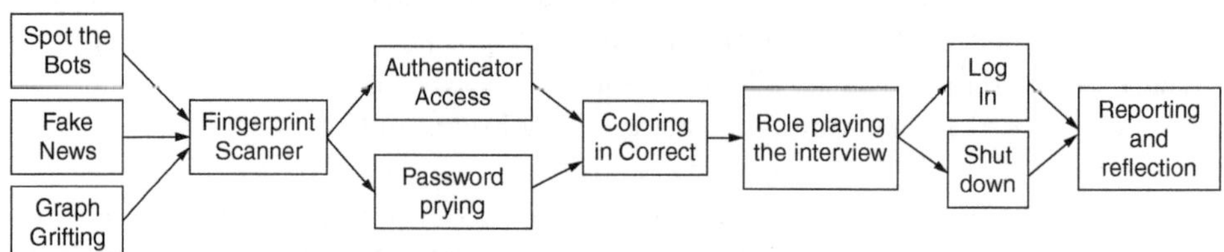

Figure 10.1 Puzzle flow diagram

There are generally two parts to a brief for an escape game. The 'Game Mechanisms Brief', which is delivered to the student, includes instructions and safety, and the 'In-Character Brief', which is delivered to the roles that the students are playing. Deliver the 'Game Mechanisms Brief' first, and invite and answer questions, so the players are ready to dive into the storyworld in the 'In-Character Brief'.

Game Mechanisms Brief:

- Provide specific directions on how players check their work. Depending on your game mode; show them how padlocks work, or instruct them to come and see you when they have solved problems, or instruct them not to open envelopes until they meet the criteria listed on the front, or direct them to the digital game.
- Provide specific directions about where the players find their initial briefing and first three challenges.
- Give any time or other constraints.
- Give any health and safety instructions, such as how players can alert you if they need something or have a concern.

In-Character Brief:
You can read this out, or film it in character:

> 'You have been working in the Information Quality Lab at the University of North England. As Information Professionals, you are called upon to stop the delivery of misinformation. Today's mission takes you into Mobius, a biotechnology lab. They have been delivering misinformation about their new project, Fingerprint Faker, out of their corporate library located at the headquarters of Mobius. The librarian is on lunch break, so you have one hour to infiltrate the library, find out what you can, and get through their fingerprint scanner.'

PART 1: IN THE LIBRARY

The library has three challenges, which can be done in any order, and a meta-challenge requiring information from all three challenges. Don't staple the sheets for a challenge together, as this will prevent players dividing up the task to solve it together; three paper clips or binder clips would be better to gather the components for each of the next three challenges. If the players are receiving everything at once, photocopy the missive and components for each challenge on a different color of paper, put them in piles, or use file folders, so that players know which pieces make up each challenge.

Setup

Self-check:
Put the fingerprint scanner that reads 'If the digits on the code add to 27, you may open this' (Figure 10.4) on a large envelope for Part 2.

Facilitated:
Give players the unlaminated sheet of fingerprints at the start. They also need access to tape and scissors as a 'fingerprint attachment kit'. Mount the fingerprint scanner that reads, 'Scan for entry' on a doorway.

Padlock:
Put the challenges for Part 2 in the largest container marked 'Scan for entry'. Use a four-digit padlock set to 8685 on the lock box. You could have a different room as this 'container'.

Components:

- opening missive from the university (Figure 10.2)
- fingerprint sheet (Figure 10.3)
    - unlaminated, along with scissors and tape if a facilitated game
    - laminated if a self-check or padlock game
- fingerprint scanner (Figure 10.4 for Self-Check, Figure 10.5 otherwise)
    - if padlocks, a four-digit padlock set to 8685.

Challenge 1a – 'Spot the Bots'

In this logic puzzle, the players will work through printouts from several social media accounts in order to separate the bots from the real people. Once they have identified the bot accounts, (Karen982, Brow4Coffee7, and Keiter119) they will look for a common location of origin. They will find that all of the locations from the bot accounts are parts of London using the user map.

Learning outcomes: players will be able to look for signs on a social media account that it is a fake account that is controlled by a computer program (a bot).

Story: the players will see how Mobius is using bot accounts to promote their products.

Skills: the players will learn authentic strategies used to identify bot accounts.

Simulation: the players will have to look at multiple sources of data in order to determine which accounts are from bots.

Components:

- 1 × 'Spot the Bots' missive from the university (Figure 10.6)
- 2 × user rosters (Figures 10.7 and 10.8)
- 1 × user maps (Figure 10.9)
- 1 × discussion forum (Figure 10.10).

Challenge 1b – Fake News

In this observational puzzle, the players will look at three printouts from the same newspaper for subtle differences in order to figure out which are fake. They will use the URLs to determine the real newspaper and compare the real newspaper to the fake. They will then learn about the Fingerprint Faker and the use of the left pinky from the faked information.

Learning outcomes: players will be able to identify some of the common ways that scammers create websites that look like news in order to fool readers.

Story: the players will learn more about the Fingerprint Faker and get a hint for another challenge through environmental storytelling.

Skills: the players will learn how to identify a false website through a URL.

Components:

- 1 × Fake News missive from the university (Figure 10.11)
- 3 × versions of The Golden Times (Figures 10.12, 10.13, and 10.14).

Challenge 1c – Graph Grifting

In this challenge, the players need to reinterpret several different types of charts (see Figures 10.16, 10.17, and 10.18) to look at the underlying data, enter the data into a sheet, and determine the most common age group for Mobius employees. Each chart gives a number of people at each of five worksites. The players need to figure out which age category is most common.

Learning outcomes: players will identify misleading graphs and learn to look beyond the graph and consider the underlying data.

Setting: graphs that were used for a job fair that were trying to mislead young job seekers. These graphs could be mounted on larger posters and put up in the room for environmental storytelling, and to give the players reason to move around the space.

Social: since this challenge has three distinct charts, each of which can be processed independently, it is good as a teamwork challenge where different players take on different charts.

Skills: players will have to look carefully at each graph and ignore the graphical presentation, looking at the underlying data instead.

Components:

- 1 × data missive from the university (Figure 10.15)
- 3 × charts (Figures 10.16, 10.17, and 10.18)
- 1 × data entry sheet (Figure 10.19).

Metapuzzle 1d: Fingerprint Scanner

The players will use the three pieces of information they got from the previous challenges (London, Left Pinky, 40–62) to find the correct fingerprint for the fingerprint scanner (8685). This is not designed to be a long challenge, as it is just the gate that ensures they have finished the three previous puzzles.

Learning outcomes:
Setting: physically engaging with a fake fingerprint helps the players to immerse more into the world of the Fingerprint Faker.

Social: players can role play taping a fake fingerprint onto their finger to scan in and scan into a reader, to engage more with their role in the world.

Facilitated:
Have the players physically engage with the challenge by having a station with scissors and tape, and requiring them to tape the fake fingerprint on to their finger and scanning it into the 'reader' (Figure 10.5), which will be taped to a door. For this, the facilitator will need to check to see if they got the correct fingerprint (8685) and have it on the left pinky, and if both are correct, then the players can be given a packet with their next set of challenges.

Padlock:
Another way to run this challenge without a facilitator is to have the fingerprint scanner attached to a box that is locked with a four-digit padlock. The players can then open

the padlock with the code 8685 to get their next set of challenges. There are several ways to facilitate this – you could give each table their own locked box, but that will encourage the players to try numbers from the sheet that is provided ahead of time. It is suggested that the box be at the front of the room, and that players are not allowed to just try number after number; this can be a good use of the 'Lock Parking Lot' concept, where players have to write down their guess, submit it to the facilitator (who can ask them how they got that number) and then are allowed to try the lock.

Self-check:
Finally, to run the challenge without a lock or a facilitator, use the 'If the digits on the code add to 27, you may open this' fingerprint scanner (Figure 10.4) placed on a large envelope. Place the rest of the game inside this envelope. This doesn't prevent players from continuing on if they choose to do so, but requires the fewest resources.

PART 2: DATA CENTER

The players enter the Data Center for Mobius. They get a message from UNE explaining that the center is being hacked and then a second message – this one from the Hackers. The players are tasked with finding the password and authenticator access code so that they can log in and allow the Hackers to get into the system, or they may instead choose to shut down the system to protect it. The players will solve two challenge, and then shift into a role-playing mode, reading scripts for a radio broadcast to give them the different perspectives, before making the final ethical choice for the game.

Learning outcomes:
Story: this is the twist, where the players are in a different location and their roles have changed from being an observer to having an active decision to make. The 'ally' of the players has changed from UNE to the Hackers, although the players have to decide if the Hackers are an ally.

Social: giving the players a difficult choice will increase the social engagement between the players, as there is no correct answer that the game is leading the players toward.

Strategic: the players imagine future scenarios and weigh up the pros and cons of their actions before proceeding.

Components:

- large envelope containing:
  - 1 × hacked missive from the university (Figure 10.20)
  - 1 × computer screen, front and back copied/glued double-sided (Figures 10.21 and 10.22)

- 7 × photographs of phone keypad with fingers (Figures 10.23 to 10.29)
- 1 × reference image of a phone keypad (Figure 10.30)
- *optional: if you would like to improve the environmental storytelling, you can print out a picture of a data center and include it in the envelope*
- if self-check, then include a small envelope with the label 'When you are CORRECT, open this envelope' (Figure 10.31) that contains Part 3.

Challenge 2a – Password Prying

The players find a memo and some notes written by a Mobius employee about changing his password. This information is attached to the back of the 'keyboard'. By looking at the pattern of previous crossed-out passwords, they can deduce what the current password is (NUYH5). The answer is that the password has been changed by moving all of the characters one space right on the keyboard each month, which is why the players are supplied with a keyboard for reference.

Learning outcomes:

Social: having the passwords on the back of the keyboard will encourage players to hold up the keyboard, and work together to communicate and solve the challenge.

Skills: players will understand why they shouldn't write their password down near the computer and to use a password-changing strategy that is more than incrementing a number.

Simulation: the players will learn how to look for a dependable pattern in how letters and numbers change, and look at their environment for clues. It also helps the players feel like a 'hacker' as they figure out someone's password.

Components:

- 1 × computer screen, front and back copied/glued double-sided (in large envelope) (Figures 10.21 and 10.22).

Challenge 2b – Authenticator Access

The players examine a series of images that were taken from a surveillance camera as the worker entered the PIN number. The images are from different times and different entries so the players need to work out the order from the timestamps, and then piece together the code (9701).

Learning outcomes: Setting: the players will see how easy it is for someone to get a PIN number when they are looking over their shoulders.

Skills: players will understand the importance of covering their hand when entering their PIN on a device.

Strategy: the players will have to determine which images are important and use different pieces of images from different times to figure out the consistent PIN. They will have to use different methods to determine some of the numbers.

Components:

- 7 × photographs of phone keypad with fingers (in large envelope) (Figures 10.23 to 10.29)
- 1 × reference image of a phone keypad (in large envelope) (Figure 10.30).

Meta-Challenge 2c: Coloring in Correct

The first step will be for the players to fill in the blanks in the 'authenticator' and 'password' fields with the letters and numbers from those challenges. In doing so, it will spell out the word 'CORRECT'. This will also be an environmental storytelling element, as it will feel like they are making the computer display appear as they enter the answers, giving them an 'a-ha' moment as they fill in the blanks. It is also feedback if they are not correct, as nothing will be spelled out.

As before, there are three ways to proceed:

Self-check: place the 'When you are CORRECT, open this envelope' label on the final small envelope that is included inside the large envelope.

Facilitated: players can bring up their filled-in CORRECT code and the facilitator can hand them the final packet.

Padlocks: use two padlocks – an alphanumeric padlock with the code NUYH5 and a four-digit padlock with the code 9701. These could be used with a hasp, so that both locks have to be opened to continue, or put two sets of holes or eyebolts into the container for both locks. These locks could also be used with the 'parking lot' concept, so that the facilitator has both locks at the front of the room. The players have to write down their guess, then show it to the facilitator and then may open the locks to get their next envelope.

Components:

- 1 × computer screen (Figures 10.21 to 10.22), front and back copied/glued double-sided and laminated with a dry-erase marker, or if unlaminated, with a marker provided (in large envelope)
  - self-check: inside the large envelope is a small envelope labelled 'Open this envelope when you are CORRECT' (Figure 10.31) and the Part 3 challenges
  - facilitated: facilitator has packets with the Part 3 challenges

    - padlocks: alphanumeric padlock with the code NUYH5 and a four-digit padlock with the code 9701, and a way to affix both to the same container, such as a hasp on a container that contains the Part 3 challenges.

PART 3: CONCLUSION AND REFLECTION

The players now move into a role-playing and reflection portion of the game. It is important at this point to remove the time pressure from the players so that they will slow down and engage with the content. This is done by giving the players a reason to stop worrying about the clock and telling them they have an important decision to make. The goal of this is to shift the players from 'solve the puzzles fast' to 'slow down and engage', and to move them into a more reflective activity.

The smaller envelope/final container should have the 'Read out loud' message, and everything needed for the last two challenges.

Components:

- Small envelope or final container with:
    - 1 × 'Read out loud' message (Figure 10.32)
    - three scripts (Radio Host, Hackers, and Mobius)
    - two sheets, each folded in half on the dotted line and taped, so that only the 'log in' and 'shut down' choices show (Figure 10.33).

Challenge 3a – Role Playing the Interview

The players now will role play a radio interview between Mobius and the Hackers. Most of this is reading from scripts, but there is space for improvisation and role play if the players want to. If they choose to only read the scripts, that will still reach the desired learning outcomes. Note: if you are running the game for one player, then play the roles of the Radio Host and of the Hackers in the role play.

Learning outcome: Social: the goal of the interview is to help the players understand both sides of this moral situation and build empathy so that they can be better informed before they make a final choice. This is a purely social challenge where players take on different roles of the factions in the story.

Components: three scripts (Radio Host, Hackers, and Mobius).

Challenge 3b – Final Choice and Reporting

Learning outcome: Story: the players get to choose the ending to their story. This makes it more personal and more powerful. Also, letting them create the ending of what happens next instead of telling them gets the players more engaged in what has happened.

Social: this is where the students come out of their groups and learn about the different experiences that other groups had.

Self: the moral choice and reflection activities are key for cementing the learning outcomes from the game.

Components:

- two sheets, each folded in half on the dotted line and taped, so that only the 'log in' and 'shut down' choices show (Figure 10.33)
- something for the players to write their 250-word reflection on and with (such as pencil and paper).

Final Reflection

Reflection is the most important part of any classroom activity, and the reflection process starts with this final challenge. The first stage of reflection is getting people to talk about what happened and how they feel about it. It is recommended for each group in class to get up and present their 250-word statement, as it will be illuminating to see how the stories are presented differently. During the reflection activities, it is important to pose questions but not provide answers; reflections are more powerful if the learner has the realization instead of being told the realization they were supposed to have had.

Here are some follow-up questions for the game. You don't need to use all of them; only choose the ones that make sense for your learning outcomes. If you have a large class, you can have the groups discuss each one first, and then have the groups present highlights from a discussion. For a smaller class, this can be an all-class discussion.

- What differences are there between the reports? Why are they different?
- What did you learn about identifying bots on social media, and how will that change your behavior?
- What did you learn about how organizations use things that appear like real news sources to misinform or sell products? How will that change your behavior?
- What did you learn about looking closely at graphs and numbers? (Show a recent example from current news that is using a misleading form of presentation.) What is wrong with this chart? How will knowing this change your behavior?
- What did you learn about PIN numbers? (Show a gas-pump skimming machine and camera set up for a real-world example.) How will this change your behavior?
- What did you learn about passwords? How will you change your passwords in the future?

- (Show companies that give you information based on your DNA.) While the concept of building a database of fingerprints for research may sound silly, there are companies now that you send off your DNA to, pay them, and they tell you about your heritage. In exchange, they get to keep the data about your DNA. What are your thoughts about this?
- What will you tell your parents that you learned from this game? If you could have them do one challenge to help them change, what would that be?
- What would you like to teach people about that you could make a challenge for? (This can be a lead-in discussion to an assignment where the students are now making their own escape games!)

COMPONENTS

We believe that key information we need is being kept under fingerprint sensor in the Mobius Library. We have procured the attached fingerprints and fingerprint attachment kit, but we **don't know which fingerprint to use, and need to know the age and location of most Mobius employees.**

Enter the library on March 28 while the librarian is on lunch break. You will have about an hour to get in, learn what you can, and get out. We have a security guard who will keep watch, and might be able to help if you need something.

We will be monitoring your progress via a camera you are wearing and will send you messages like this one as you discover interesting information.

Figure 10.2 Mobius Library, opening missive from the university

Finger	Left Pinky	Left Ring	Left Middle	Left Fore	Right Fore	Right Middle	Right Ring	Right Pinky
NYC 18–25	2834	9538	8824	7391	6109	5501	4054	3903
NYC 26–39	1721	1098	9098	8560	7447	6043	3101	2287
NYC 40–62	3926	2064	1385	9832	8927	7827	2897	1799
London 18–25	4149	3077	2543	1742	9764	8454	1865	0273
London 26–39	5003	4092	3467	2199	1108	9002	5522	9462
London 40–62	8685	5019	4183	3756	2312	0457	6391	6938
Sing. 18–25	7293	6603	5058	4009	3760	1067	7010	7341
Sing. 26–39	8229	7453	6276	5098	4002	2842	8343	6023
Sing. 40–62	9086	8392	7653	6367	5973	3457	9434	5023

Figure 10.3 Library, fingerprint sheet

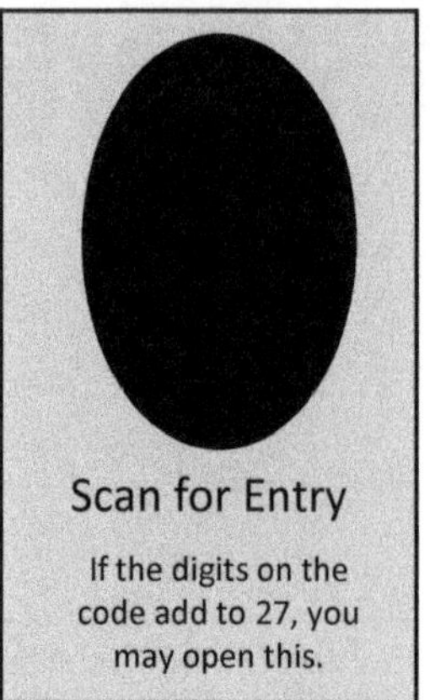

Figure 10.4 Library, self-check fingerprint scanner

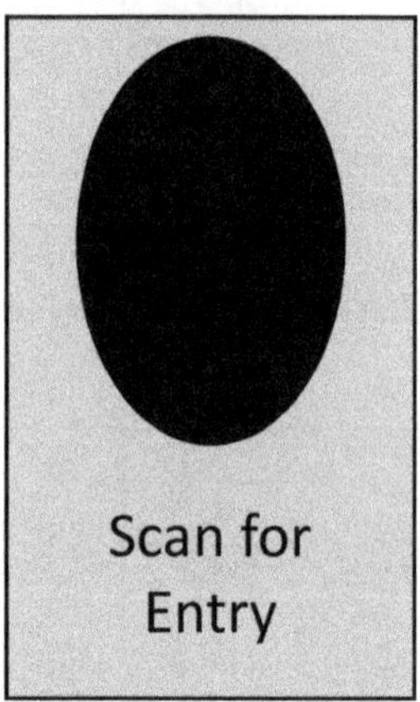

Figure 10.5 Library, facilitated and padlocks fingerprint scanner

We have learned that Mobius has created three chat programs known as bots to send messages on the social media platform Handbook to raise panic with false stories about fingerprint theft.
Here are the aspects to look for to spot the bots:

1: Bots have automatically generated names, so most have a number as part of their user name or a set of words put together that don't make much sense.
2: Bots copy their profile pictures from other profiles, so look for duplicated icons. They may also take profile text from other profiles, so look for copied phrases.
3: Bots may re-post content and follow many people, but may not have many other followers.

Once you have identified the three bots, see if you can find where they are coming from.

Figure 10.6 Library challenge 1a, Spot the Bots missive from the university

Figure 10.7 Library challenge 1a, user roster (1 of 2)

Handbook				User roster			
Name	**Icon**	**Hometown**	**About me**	**Posts**	**Re-posts**	**Following**	**Followers**
Robert27		Queens	48, married, two kids, sell insurance, watches sports on weekends. Go Dodgers!	3	4	83	4
RobotsRCool		Changi	E-sports enthusiast and K-pop fan. Love robot battles!	12	24	112	74
Gh0sty117Red		Brooklyn	Unemployed actress, unemployed waitress, unemployed everything. Looking for any work near Brooklyn.	53	12	35	28
Karen982		Brixton	Single, 29, hot, looking for lonely men.	3	83	71	21

Figure 10.8 Library challenge 1a, user roster (2 of 2)

Handbook				User roster			
Name	**Icon**	**Hometown**	**About me**	**Posts**	**Re-posts**	**Following**	**Followers**
Smithore2012		Bronx	Whatever, nobody reads this anyway.	1	0	12	1
Brow4Coffee7		Hampstead	I enjoy the internet and reading the many fine posts from handbook. Please message me!	2	28	52	3
AileeRoberts		Rochor	Single, 29, looking for someone to share chili crab with. Tired of living alone.	42	3	112	53
Keiter119		Newham	Unemployed actress, two kids, sells insurance. Loves robot battles!	4	38	173	10

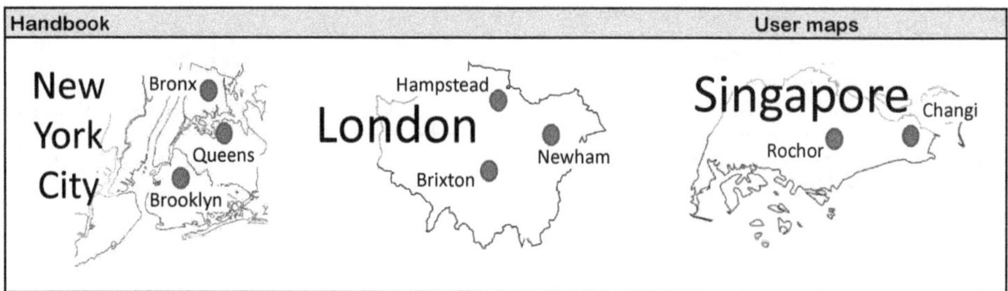

Figure 10.9 Library challenge 1a, user map

Figure 10.10 Library challenge 1a, discussion forum

Handbook			**Discussion forum**
	AileeRoberts	March 3, 2021, 18:42	Hey, is anyone free tonight near Singapore? I'd love to go out and get something to eat and talk.
	Robert27	March 3, 2021, 19:23	➥Would love to, but am a little far away. LOL.
	Gh0sty117Red	March 4, 2021, 9:30	Up early again. No work yet, but can't sleep in. Can't put my finger on why.
	Keiter119	March 4, 2021, 9:31	➥Speaking of fingers, did you see this story about people faking fingerprints?
	Gh0sty117Red	March 4, 2021, 9:43	➥That is scary stuff! How do I get my fingerprint off my phone?
	Karen982	March 4, 2021, 9:41	➥There's a service from Mobius where you can buy a fake fingertip kit. I use it. It's great! #safetyfirst ⮝Robert27,Keiter119 Re-posted this
	Gh0sty117Red	March 4, 2021, 9:51	➥Thanks, I will check that out!
	RobotsRCool	March 4, 2021, 11:51	Did anyone see last night's Robot Wars? It was awesome! Parts were flying everywhere! ⮝Karen982 Re-posted this
	Brow4Coffee7	March 4, 2021, 11:52	➥LOL. Please message me!

(Continued)

Figure 10.10 Library challenge 1a, discussion forum *(Continued)*

Handbook		Discussion forum	
	Keiter119	March 4, 2021, 1:31	Speaking of fingers, did you see this story about people faking fingerprints? ▲Karen982 Re-posted this
	Karen982	March 4, 2021, 1:31	➥There's a service from Mobius where you can buy a fake fingertip kit. I use it. It's great! #safetyfirst
	Brow4Coffee7	March 4, 2021, 11:52	➥LOL. Please message me!
	Smithore2012	March 4, 2021, 12:43	Man, did anyone see that story about the fake fingerprints that is going around the internet? Scary stuff!
	Keiter119	March 4, 2021, 1:31	Speaking of fingers, did you see this story about people faking fingerprints? ▲ Karen982 Re-posted this
	Karen982	March 4, 2021, 1:31	➥There's a service from Mobius where you can buy a fake fingertip kit. I use it. It's great! #safetyfirst

Mobius has been spreading fake website that look like a real newspaper. Examine each of these printouts from newspaper website to determine which is real and which is fake, and compare them to figure out what Mobius has been trying to do and what finger is important. Start by analyzing the URL of the website to determine if the website is real or fake.

Figure 10.11 Library challenge 1b, Fake News missive from the university

←→↺ http://goldentimes.com.honesttruth.com

THE GOLDEN TIMES

http://goldentimes.com Online Edition

FINGERPRINTS AT RISK

Unlocking your phone with your fingerprint?

It might be convenient, but you may be giving away more than you think when you unlock your phone with your fingerprint. The International Crime Commission reports a spike in identity theft crimes enabled by the criminals wearing false fingertips to copy their victims.

"It may save you two seconds when you swipe with your fingertip, but can cost you years of recovery if your online identity is copied," says Thomas Smithdol, head of Forensic Impersonation for the (ICC) International Crime Commission.

Smithdol recommends that people use a more complex version of biometric measures, such as facial identification, or return to using a PIN code on their phones.

If they must use a fingerprint scan, Smithdol recommends people use a fake fingerprint on their left pinky. "The right index finger is the most commonly used finger for these fingerprint scans. Using a left pinky fake fingerprint from a trusted company like Mobius will ensure your data is safe."

Lonely in your Golden Years?
Find other seniors seeking companionship through Ember.com. Don't journey through the best years of your life alone.
Paid advertisement

Figure 10.12 Library challenge 1b, The Golden Times (1 of 3)

←→↺ http://goldentimes.com

THE GOLDEN TIMES

http://goldentimes.com Online Edition

FINGERPRINTS AT RISK

Unlocking your phone with your fingerprint?

It might be convenient, but you may be giving away more than you think when you unlock your phone with your fingerprint. The International Crime Commission reports a spike in identity theft crimes enabled by the criminals wearing false fingertips to copy their victims.

"It may save you two seconds when you swipe with your fingertip, but can cost you years of recovery if your online identity is copied," says Thomas Smithdol, head of Forensic Impersonation for the (ICC) International Crime Commission.

Smithdol recommends that people use a more complex version of biometric measures, such as facial identification, or return to using a PIN code on their phones.

If they must use a fingerprint scan, Smithdol recommends people avoid using their index finger. "The right index finger is the most commonly used finger for these fingerprint scans. If you use the same right index finger on multiple devices, then that sets the stage for a criminal to take that information and impersonate you online."

Lonely in your Golden Years?
Find other seniors seeking companionship through Ember.com. Don't journey through the best years of your life alone.
Paid advertisement

Figure 10.13 Library challenge 1b, The Golden Times (2 of 3)

←→↺ http://g∅ldentimes.com

THE GOLDEN TIMES

http://goldentimes.com Online Edition

FINGERPRINTS AT RISK

Be Safe with Fingerprint Faker

Studies show that people who use Fingerprint Faker from Mobius are 95% less likely to be taken advantage of. Order your custom-fit Fingerprint Faker at http://mobius.uk/fingerprintfaker

Unlocking your phone with your fingerprint?

It might be convenient, but you may be giving away more than you think when you unlock your phone with your fingerprint. The International Crime Commission reports a spike in identity theft crimes enabled by the criminals wearing false fingertips to copy their victims.

"It may save you two seconds when you swipe with your fingertip, but can cost you years of recovery if your online identity is copied," says Thomas Smithdol, head of Forensic Impersonation for the (ICC) International Crime Commission.

Smithdol recommends that people use a more complex version of biometric measures, such as facial identification, or return to using a PIN code on their phones.

If they must use a fingerprint scan, Smithdol recommends people avoid using their index finger. "The right index finger is the most commonly used finger for these fingerprint scans. If you use the same right index finger on multiple devices, then that sets the stage for a criminal to take that information and impersonate you online."

Figure 10.14 Library challenge 1b, The Golden Times (3 of 3)

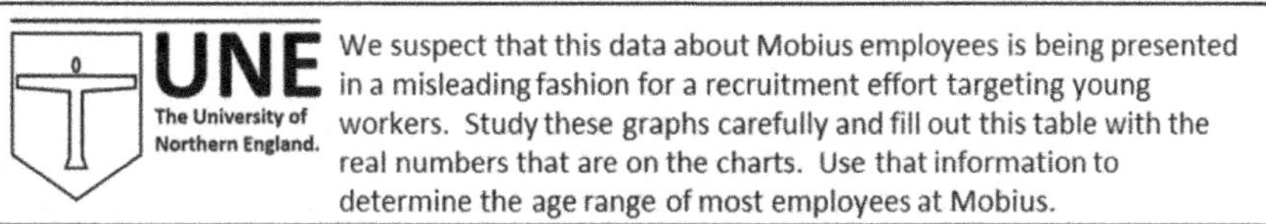

UNE The University of Northern England.

We suspect that this data about Mobius employees is being presented in a misleading fashion for a recruitment effort targeting young workers. Study these graphs carefully and fill out this table with the real numbers that are on the charts. Use that information to determine the age range of most employees at Mobius.

Figure 10.15 Library challenge 1c, data missive from the university

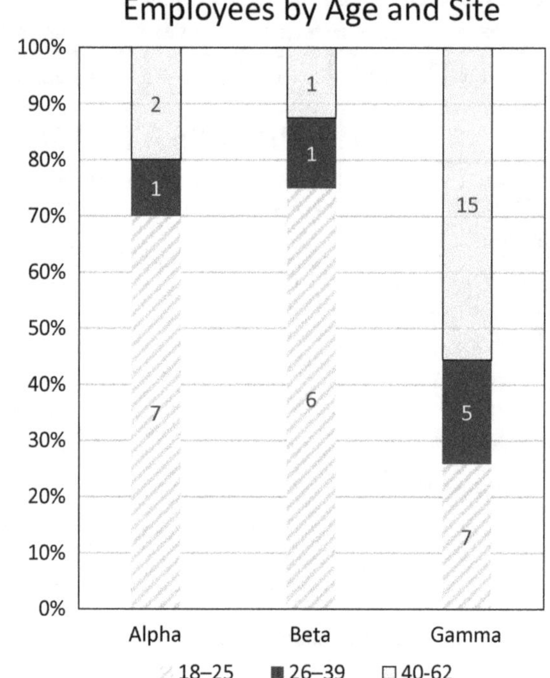

Figure 10.16 Library challenge 1c, chart (1 of 3)

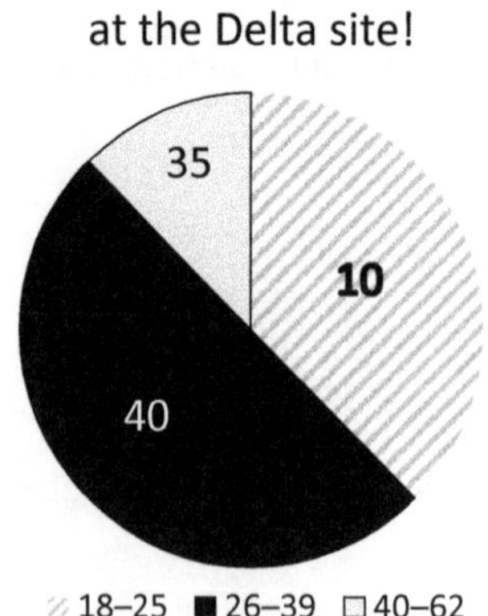

Figure 10.17 Library challenge 1c, chart (2 of 3)

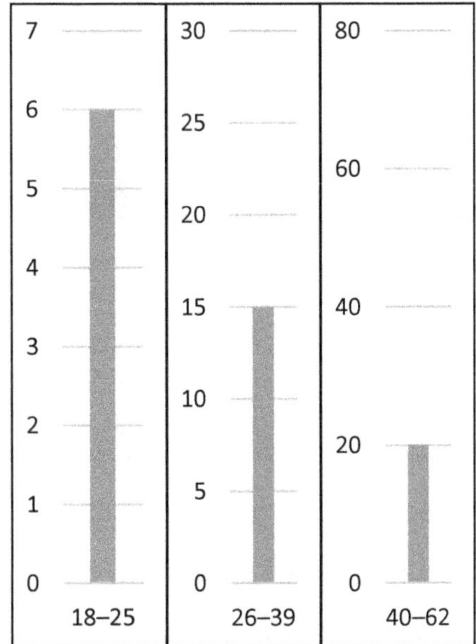

Figure 10.18 Library challenge 1c, chart (3 of 3)

Employee Census

	18-25	26-39	40-62
Alpha			
Beta			
Gamma			
Delta			
Epsilon			
TOTALS:			

Figure 10.19 Library challenge 1c, data entry sheet

UNE The University of Northern England.

We can see you are surrounded by computers – You have found the Data Center for Mobius! Great work!

We have been monitoring an internet forum that is actively planning a hack on the fingerprint database at Mobius, which would give them access to hundreds of thousands of fingerprints. We can see from the main screen that the hack is in process. You need to @&#$)&@((@))8)@)_#>><?>?>#

WE HAVE INTERRUPTED THIS MESSAGE. WE ARE THE ONES HACKING MOBIUS.

WE PLAN TO DELETE THEIR DATABASES ONCE WE HAVE ACCESS.
IT IS IMPERATIVE THAT YOU **LOG IN** TO LET US HAVE ACCESS.

DO NOT SHUT DOWN.

WE ARE TRANSMITTING IMAGES OF THE KEYPAD FOR THE AUTHENTICATOR. THEY DID NOT COVER THEIR HAND WHEN ENTERING THEIR 4-DIGIT PIN.

THE PASSWORD IS CHANGED REGULARLY AND KEPT UNDER THE KEYBOARD.

AFTER YOU FILL IN THE AUTHENTICATOR AND PASSWORD ON THE COMPUTER, CHOOSE LOG IN TO GIVE US ACCESS. DO NOT SHUT DOWN THE COMPUTER.

WE ARE WATCHING.

Figure 10.20 Data Center, hacked missive from the university

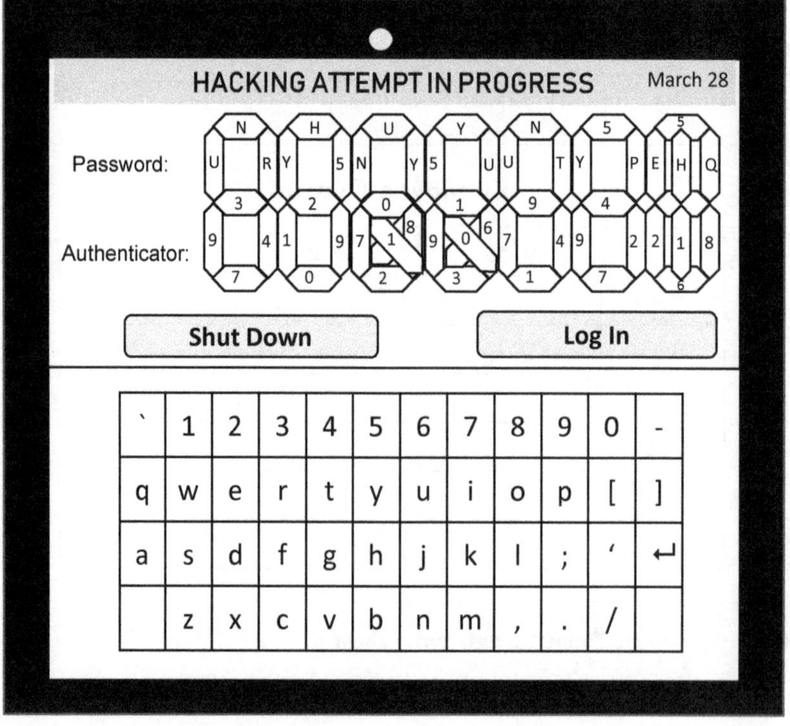

Figure 10.21 Data Center, challenge 2a, computer screen (front)

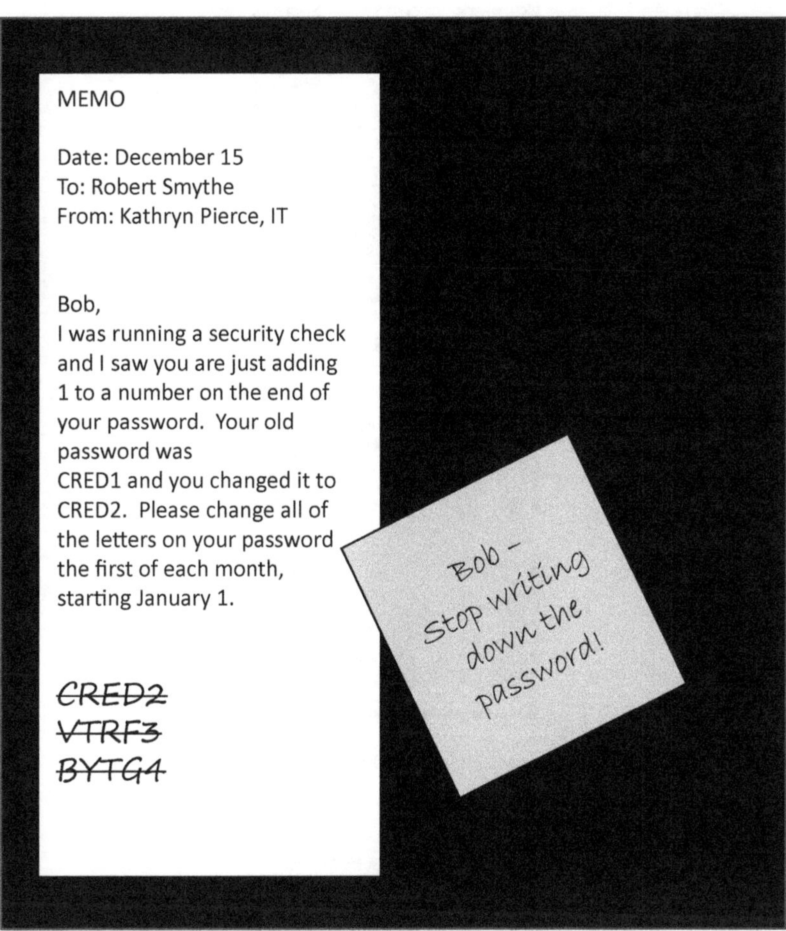
MEMO

Date: December 15
To: Robert Smythe
From: Kathryn Pierce, IT

Bob,
I was running a security check and I saw you are just adding 1 to a number on the end of your password. Your old password was CRED1 and you changed it to CRED2. Please change all of the letters on your password the first of each month, starting January 1.

~~CRED2~~
~~VTRF3~~
~~BYTG4~~

Figure 10.22 Data Center, challenge 2a, computer screen (back)

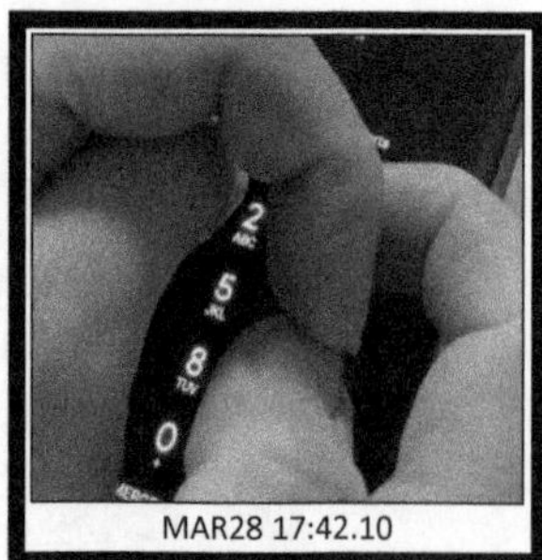

Figure 10.23 Data Center, challenge 2b, phone keypad (1 of 7)

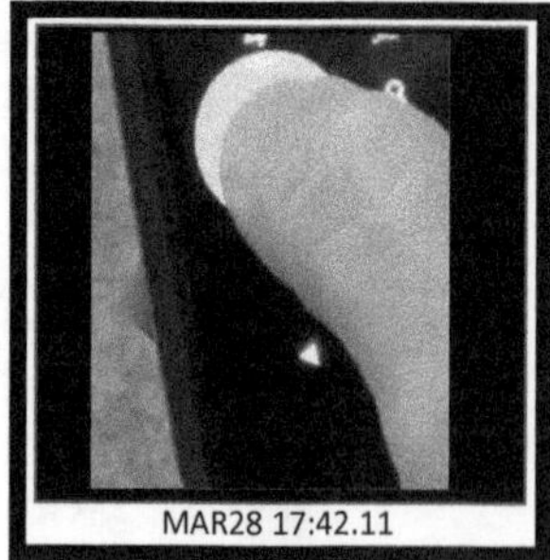

Figure 10.24 Data Center, challenge 2b, phone keypad (2 of 7)

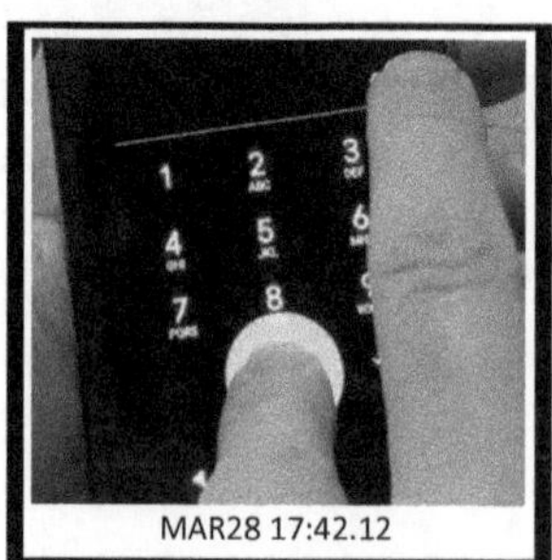

Figure 10.25 Data Center, challenge 2b, phone keypad (3 of 7)

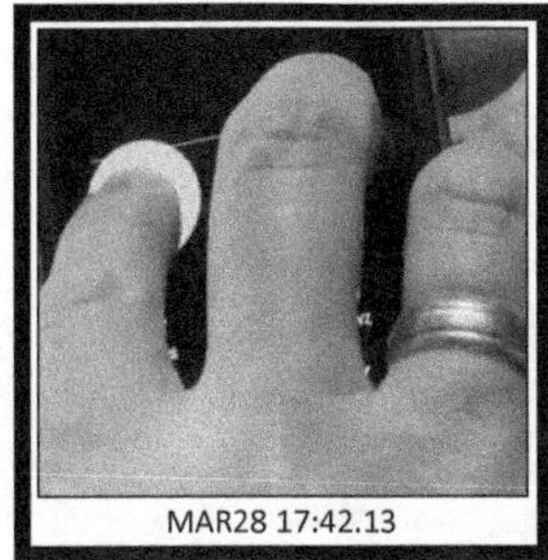

Figure 10.26 Data Center, challenge 2b, phone keypad (4 of 7)

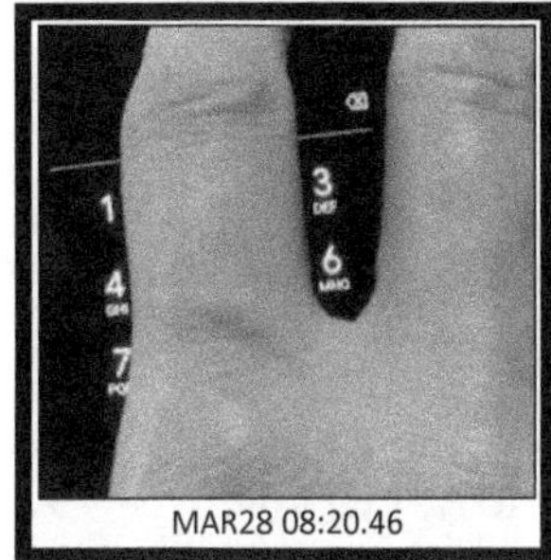

Figure 10.27 Data Center, challenge 2b, phone keypad (5 of 7)

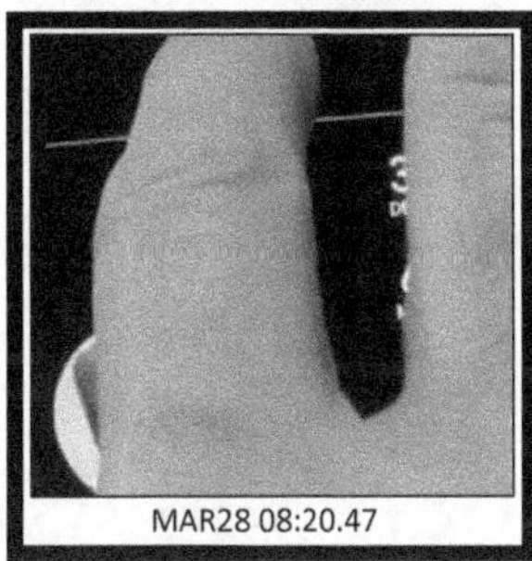

Figure 10.28 Data Center, challenge 2b, phone keypad (6 of 7)

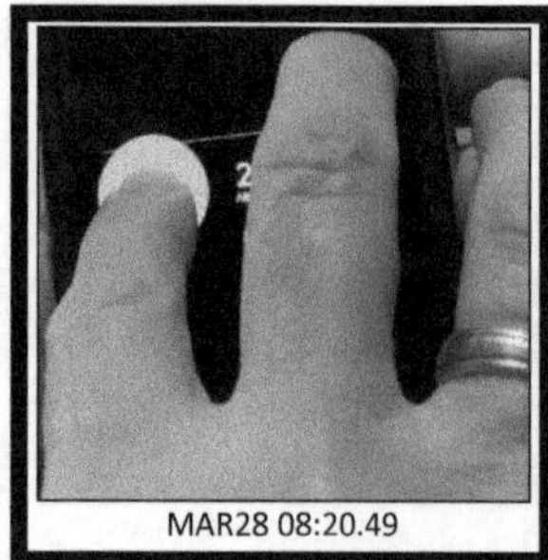

Figure 10.29 Data Center, challenge 2b, phone keypad (7 of 7)

Figure 10.30 Data Center, challenge 2b, reference phone keypad

WHEN YOU ARE
CORRECT
OPEN THIS
ENVELOPE

Figure 10.31 Data Center, 'When you are correct' label for small envelope

Read Out Loud

Congratulations! You figured out the password and authenticator but realize you are faced with a difficult decision. You tell the guard to find the librarian and keep them from coming back, so you can take your time and make the right decision.

As you finish entering the password and authenticator code, a radio broadcast starts to play over your communication device. It is an interview between Mobius and the Hackers.

Decide who will be the Radio Host, who will play Mobius, and who will play the Hackers. Everyone else is the audience and will ask questions. Distribute the enclosed scripts. The Radio Host will direct the interview by following the script. Mobius and the Hackers can improvise answers based upon the information they have.

Figure 10.32 Conclusion, 'Read out loud' message

Assembly Instructions:
Cut on the dark lines. Fold upward using the dotted line and seal with tape, leaving the Log In and Shut Down choices visible.

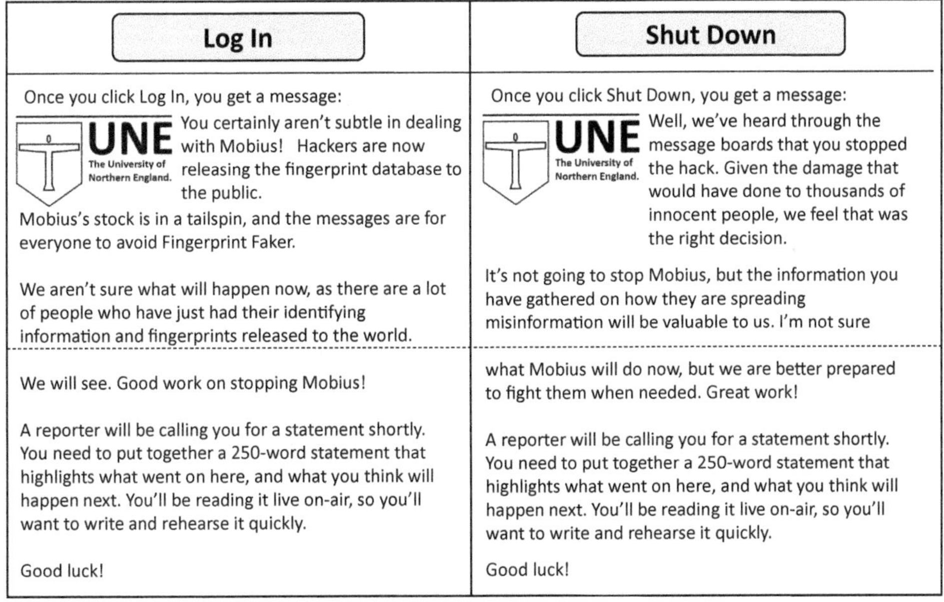

Log In	Shut Down
Once you click Log In, you get a message: UNE The University of Northern England. You certainly aren't subtle in dealing with Mobius! Hackers are now releasing the fingerprint database to the public. Mobius's stock is in a tailspin, and the messages are for everyone to avoid Fingerprint Faker. We aren't sure what will happen now, as there are a lot of people who have just had their identifying information and fingerprints released to the world.	Once you click Shut Down, you get a message: UNE The University of Northern England. Well, we've heard through the message boards that you stopped the hack. Given the damage that would have done to thousands of innocent people, we feel that was the right decision. It's not going to stop Mobius, but the information you have gathered on how they are spreading misinformation will be valuable to us. I'm not sure
We will see. Good work on stopping Mobius! A reporter will be calling you for a statement shortly. You need to put together a 250-word statement that highlights what went on here, and what you think will happen next. You'll be reading it live on-air, so you'll want to write and rehearse it quickly. Good luck!	what Mobius will do now, but we are better prepared to fight them when needed. Great work! A reporter will be calling you for a statement shortly. You need to put together a 250-word statement that highlights what went on here, and what you think will happen next. You'll be reading it live on-air, so you'll want to write and rehearse it quickly. Good luck!

Figure 10.33 Conclusion, final choice message

SCRIPT – RADIO HOST

To start, read out loud:

> Welcome to our live radio interview with Mobius. We have learned that a group of Hackers are about to get into Mobius's systems as we speak, so we have brought the Hackers on as well.

Q: Hackers, tell us what is happening and why?

[Wait for answer.]

Q: Mobius, what are you going to do with all of those fingerprints?

[Wait for answer.]

Q: Hackers, what will you do with the fingerprint database?

[Wait for answer.]

Q: Mobius, what impact would this have on you?

[Wait for answer.]

Now let's turn this over to our studio audience. What questions do you have?

[Facilitate questions and answers. You may also ask questions.]

Well, that's all the time we have. Thank you for joining us.

[Dramatic pause, then read this in your best movie announcer voice.]

Now, it is back to our heroes. They are faced with a choice. Do they shut down the system and keep the data safe, or do they log on and allow the hackers access? They have a few moments to debate and then must make a decision.

[Find the sealed sheets labeled 'Log On' and 'Shut Down', and put them in the middle of the table.]

SCRIPT – HACKERS

When asked about what is happening:
We are just about to complete a hack into Mobius's fingerprint database. They have collected thousands of fingerprints for their Fingerprint Faker, and that is far too much power. We have live video and a team on the inside who is about to break in to the system!

When asked about what they will do:
We will release this fingerprint database to the world! That way, anyone who wants to do research on fingerprints can do so. This will force those using fingerprints to come up with another way to validate identities, as fingerprints will become easily copied and useless. If everyone has access to fingerprints, then nobody can use them for control.

If asked about innocent people:
You can't fight an information war without casualties. In the short term, it will be inconvenient for the customers, but these are people who already have tried to cheat the system by ordering the Fingerprint Faker in the first place! It will be worth it in the end.

SCRIPT – MOBIUS

When asked about what Mobius will do with the fingerprints:
Our Fingerprint Faker is designed to protect people from hackers like these. We use the fingerprints for research, so that we can improve our product with a larger database of fingerprints.

When asked about what impact this would have:
We still have the fingerprint data, so it won't affect our research. All this action will do is put the identities of thousands of people at risk. If you release these fingerprints, think about the consequences it will have for our customers, and for what benefit? This will do much more harm than it will do good.

If asked about future products:
Our next product will be DNA Denier, which is similar to Fingerprint Faker, but for DNA testing. This will provide people with an artificial DNA that is similar to their own, but with some changes made, to protect them from invasive DNA testing.

CHECKLIST

Start players with: Opening missive (Figure 10.2), fingerprint sheet (Figure 10.3), scissors and tape (if using).

Part 1

Prepare three packets (place separate areas of the room or use different colors of paper):

- 'Spot the Bots' missive (Figure 10.6), user rosters (2) (Figures 10.7 and 10.8), user map (Figure 10.9), and discussion forum (Figure 10.10)
- Fake News missive (Figure 10.11), news web pages (3) (Figures 10.12, 10.13, and 10.14).
- Graph Grifting missive (Figure 10.15), charts (3) (Figures 10.16, 10.17, and 10.18), data entry sheet (Figure 10.19).

Prepare one of the following:

- Self-check: 'Scan for entry with sum of 27' (Figure 10.4) on large envelope
- Facilitated: 'Scan for entry' (Figure 10.5) on doorway
- Padlock: 'Scan for entry' (Figure 10.5) on large container with four-digit lock set to 8685

Part 2

Large envelope/container with:

- Hacked missive (Figure 10.20), computer screen copied front-to-back (Figures 10.21 and 10.22).
- Authenticator (Figure 10.30), seven pictures of PIN entry (Figures 10.23-10.29).

Prepare one of the following:

- Self-check: 'When you are CORRECT' message (Figure 10.31) on small envelope.
- Padlock: small container with five alphanumeric padlocks set to NUYH5, and a four-digit padlock set to 9701.
- Facilitated: small envelope ready to be handed out.

Part 3

Small envelope with:

- Read out loud message (Figure 10.32), scripts for Radio Host, Hackers, and Mobius (3)
- Log in and shut down sheets (Figure 10.33), cut apart, folded, and taped.

Game Master's Guide

The goal of this document is that it is something to carry with you during the game as a key for each of the puzzles to provide a quick reference to help players who are struggling.

1a – Spot the Bots – Answer: London

Bots are:

Karen982 (copied profile, many re-posts, promoting Mobius with the same message).

Brow4Coffee7 (many re-posts, high # of following, replies with the same message).

Keiter119 (copied profile, high # of following, links to same post several times).

All three are from cities on the London map.

1b – Fake News – Answer: Left Pinky

Real post has URL of http://goldentimes.com. Fake posts have URLs of http://gØldentimes.com and http://goldentimes.com.honesttruth.com, which contains instructions from Mobius to use Left Pinky.

1c – Graft Grifting – Answer: 40–62

Table 10.1 Answer Key for Graph Grifting

ANSWER KEY	18-25	26-39	40-62
Alpha	7	1	2
Beta	6	1	1
Gamma	7	5	15
Delta	10	40	35
Epsilon	6	15	20
Totals	36	62	73

1d – Fingerprint Scanner – Answer: 8685

London + Left Pinky + 40–62

2a – Password Prying – Answer: NUYH5

Move to the right on the keyboard one character from the previous password.

2b – Authenticator Access – Answer: 9701

Put the time stamps in order for two sets of pictures. One has four pictures, the other is missing #3.

First digit (9) – Eliminate 2580 from one picture and 14736 from the other picture, leaving 9.

Second digit (7) – It's between the four and eight, so must be the seven.

Third digit (0) – Clearly a 0 in the single picture available for the number.

Fourth digit (1) – Top left digit, next to the two.

2c – Coloring in CORRECT – Answers: NUYH5 and 9701

By coloring in the spots corresponding to the letters and numbers, the player gets CORRECT.

GAME DESIGN NOTES

When I sat down to design the game, I started by developing a set of learning outcomes to explore. The first question I considered was if I wanted to take one learning outcome and explore it in-depth, or take several different learning outcomes and touch on each. I decided on the second, with the intention that a teacher would then use this game as the starting point for further discussions on each of the topic areas – fake news, bots on social media, misleading charts, password safety, and PIN safety. As I do in most of my games, I also wanted to pose an ethical question for the players to consider and wanted to give the players a meaningful choice during the game.

For the game structure, I knew I wanted the game to have some flexibility, which is why there is a midway stopping point, so that the game could be run in two 30-minute sections. It could be restructured further and run challenge-by-challenge over a series of weeks, but I didn't want to add another version to the script. I also wanted to demonstrate different methods for resolving challenges, both with and without padlocks, to help designers have more examples of different ways to gate content.

Spot the Bots

I started by coming up with the things that the bots will do that are suspicious:

- Following up on other posts with similarly worded content in short timeframes.

- All following each other.
- Copying parts of profiles from other users.
- Having suspicious names with numbers.
- Having high numbers of posts, re-posts but few followers.

I then needed to decide upon how many bots and how many real profiles we would have. This is where the puzzle length will be set, as the larger this pool, the longer it will take to solve the puzzle. This should not be a long puzzle, so I settled on three bots and five real profiles, but would emphasize the bot behavior in the discussion forum.

The next step was to create the fake social media spaces. The original concept was to create a profile for each user, but this introduced too many potential red herrings and distractors. Using a more simplified user database allowed us to focus the information on what the players needed. Then, I thought about the goal of the challenge – to introduce the players to bots and learn some of their common traits. To accomplish this, the challenge does not need to be too onerous; the bots' behavior was blatant, so that the players can easily spot them. It is tempting to get creative and tricky at this point to make the players hunt for details, but that's not in line with the learning outcomes.

Fake News

First, I created the 'real' newspaper. I limited the content so as not to overwhelm the player, but by using the title 'The Golden Times' and the ad for a seniors' dating service, created environmental storytelling to indicate that the person who had these papers and the primary targets are older. I researched what to look for in a fake web address and used two of the common practices to create false URLs. Then, reflecting reality, I made small changes to the false newspapers – changing the advertisement in one and changing the text in another. I also made sure the changes accomplished the goals in our tasks – one change conveyed to the players which finger to use, and the other to immerse the players into the world created for the story.

Graph Grifting

I first identified three ways that graphical data is used to hide underlying patterns in the real number. I also made sure to include the actual numbers with the graphical images so that the players had what they needed to solve the challenges. I then needed to come up with a story as to why these charts were there, as they don't really fit into the Fingerprint Faker story in a way that then would make sense for the meta-challenge of figuring out the right fingerprint to use. This challenge, therefore, does not contribute to the Fingerprint Faker narrative like the other two do. Instead, this challenge better establishes the world of Mobius.

More importantly, this story element provides a goal with each chart to make the chart appear to favor the younger demographic while hiding the reality. I also didn't want to make it obvious with one chart what was going on, so that they would need to analyze each chart. The table (Figure 10.19) is not required, but I found in testing that players were more likely to systematically go through everything if they had a table that they were completing.

Fingerprint Scanner

It is important that everything we put together fits in the narrative world, so I needed to think of a reason that a four-digit lock would make sense here. Tying it into the narrative of a specific code for a fingerprint then allowed us to have a more immersive activity or a more role-playing-based activity. One of the disadvantages of this method of a look-up table is that it is easy to 'brute force' the answer after the players have figured out which finger it is; this is why we suggest the one communal lock instead of the individual locks. To avoid this, I would create three tables, one for each of the categories, that would give part of a fingerprint and a number. The players could then add the three numbers together to get a total, which would give them the lock code. But this adds complexity and isn't realistic, so I chose the simpler path of a large look-up table.

Another layer that a facilitator could add here could be a 'laser beam maze' protecting the scanner. By stringing yarn with small bells attached across the entry to the door, it will add a physical challenge to the game. To allow everyone a chance to try this, it could be set up in a hallway and the entire team has to work through the maze to continue. This is not an official part of the game, but if there is a desire to add more of a spy feel to the game, this would be a good place to do that.

Password Prying

To create this challenge, I had to craft the situation where it made sense for someone to write down previous passwords, but not have the current password written down. This is where we used environmental storytelling with the memo, the handwritten crossed-out passwords, and the post-it note to help players piece together what has happened. Note that even though this challenge does not advance the main narrative, it is developed around its own consistent narrative, which is where the environmental storytelling leads into the players solving the challenge.

While I could have used a more traditional cipher method for this challenge, that didn't make sense for the situation. Someone who was lazy and didn't really want to change their password wouldn't go to the trouble of using a pigpen cipher or a Morse code cipher. However, using the method of just moving your hands over one set of keys on a keyboard is a lazy way to change something without having to think about it.

The players need to see a keyboard to solve the puzzle. Rather than use a picture of a standard keyboard, which would have worked, we created a 'keyboard' that doesn't look quite right. This is signposting, as it is giving the players a hint that something is going on with this keyboard. By putting the password information on the 'back' of the keyboard, it creates a communication challenge to allow the team to work together.

Authenticator Access

Starting with the learning outcome, I used the design model of 'flip the script', where the players play the bad guys in a situation to help them understand the threats. This puzzle combines 'a-ha' and process moments, and is solved in multiple stages. In the first stage, the players realize they have seven pictures but need four digits, so something is unusual. By looking at the time stamps, they can see that the pictures come from two different times and there is a skip in the sequence of one of the sets of pictures. This lets the players have the first 'a-ha', that the third digit is missing in one of the sequences.

This then moves into a process puzzle, where the players can confirm digits two, three, and four relatively easily. If they struggle with figuring out the seven, they can compare the picture to the picture that is provided of the Authenticator keypad to see where the seven would be.

But then the puzzle requires another 'a-ha' around the first digit, as there is no definite circle showing which digit is correct. This requires a different way of thinking, as the players have to use logic and the process of elimination to decide the only digit that it could be in both pictures is a nine. Therefore, this puzzle requires different modes of thought and several 'a-has' to solve.

By having so little visual information, but still being able to figure out the PIN, this will reinforce the learning outcome that covering your hand while you enter your PIN is important.

Role-Playing Activity

When providing players with a choice, it is important that they have some background with which to make that choice. If the players aren't provided with multiple perspectives, they will come in with the perspective they already had and won't be encouraged to consider other perspectives. Forcing players to 'play a role' will help at least that player to have empathy for that perspective in the situation. The goal is to encourage players to have a discussion about the moral choice, and seeding that discussion with a script will move people in that way. By providing players with a script to read, it will ensure that anyone can be involved in the 'role playing' without having to act or improvise, but there is space allowed for improvisation for players who enjoy that.

Final Choice and Reporting

Just as the prior activity changed the stage, this activity changes the stage yet again. By doing this, it forces the players to step back from their active role and examine what went on. Creating the tight 250-word limit means that players must focus on what was most important for them during the experience. Sharing these ensures that everyone will benefit from the experiences that others had. The process of moving into reflection is a critical time to calm down, step away from the timers and rewards, and reflect upon how this game changed the players. Do not short change the reflection process, as this is how learning happens.

INDEX

3D printer, 122

A1Z26 cipher, 98
affordances, 47–8
a–ha (in puzzles), 36, 71, 76, 78, 89, 121
assessment, 136–140
audio, 111, 127

backsolving, 36–7, 103
books, 98–9, 109–110
Braille, 98
breakout box *see* puzzle box
Breakout EDU, 29, 42
  see also puzzle box
briefing players, 58, 110–112, 124, 127
blacklight *see* UV light

Caesar substitution cipher, 97–8
cipher, 97–9
challenge, 2–3, 59–60
checklists, 128
clues *see* hints
codes *see* encoding messages
costumes, 100, 101, 112
crosswords, 64–5, 86–7
cryptography, 97–9
conflict, 50–1, 53, 55
construction, 121–2
containers, 4, 27, 29–31, 74, 108–110, 121
Csíkszentmihályi, Mihály, 115–116

debriefing *see* reflection
deduction puzzles, 93–4
design process, 60
Dewey, John, 132–3
digital tools, 37, 42–3, 74
distractors, 80

Einstein puzzle, 89–91
encoding messages, 97–9
environmental storytelling, 59, 110–112
escape game (definition) 1, 25
escape rooms, 2–4, 25
  commercial, 5, 13, 15–16, 45, 106, 113
  social, 21
event preparation, 128, 131, 171–4
experience design, 105
exposition, 56, 58–9

facilitation, 128, 130–2
  see also hints, feedback, reflection
factual puzzles, 65, 86–7
feedback
  about performance, 131 134–6
  in puzzle design, 68–70, 78, 92, 121
Flow (theory of), 115–8
framework, 8

game shapes, 5–6, 25
game master
  see facilitation
game props (creating), 121–2
gates, 4, 97, 106–110
genre, 46–7, 57–8
groups, 11

hasp, 29–30, 106–7
hints 10, 12, 13, 14–5, 16–7, 18–9, 20, 22–3, 94, 130–2
hybrid games, 40–1

inquiry–based learning, 13, 17

jigsaw method (team organization), 49–50

knowledge types, 8–9
Kohn, Alfie, 114–5

layers (adding), 75–8, 80, 117
LARP *see* Live–Action Role–Playing
laser cutter, 122
LATCH (theory), 76
learner–developed games, 137–9
learning objectives, 7
learning outcomes, 7, 35, 48, 55–6, 63, 137–8
  math–based, 95–6
  and puzzle design, 81, 86, 88
  and role–playing, 100
  selecting appropriate, 113–114
  using to add layers, 75
letter–number cipher, 98
linear games, 64, 106
lighting, 110–111
Live–Action Role–Playing (LARP), 2,99–102
locks, 27, 29–30, 31, 70–1, 72–5, 107;
  parking lot 30
logic puzzles, 89–93

maps, 66–7
math puzzles, 95–6
mega–escape game, 41, 102
metapuzzles, 18, 35–6, 102–3, 106
minimum viable prototype, 119–120
Morse code, 98
mystery, 19, 93–4

narrative
  see story
non–linear games, 64, 102, 106
  and learning outcomes, 106–7
Non–Player Character (NPC), 3, 13, 15, 27, 51, 58–9, 127, 130
NPC *see* Non–Player Character

obfuscation, 37
observational puzzles, 31–2, 88–9, 100–1, 109
one–box wonder, 32, 88–9

padlocks *see* locks
prototyping, 119–120, 121–122
pigpen cipher, 125
pop–up escape room, 25, 26–8
physical activity, 3, 37
physical space, 9, 26–7, 31–2 108, 110–112
playtesting, 78–9, 120–1, 124–8
Polybius square cipher, 98
process, 36, 80–1
puzzles
  adjusting 79–81, 120–1, 126
  changing the scale, 122–3
  components, 65
  creation, 63–5, 78, 123
  definition, 63
  flow diagram, 31, 34, 144
  goals, 70–2
  for learning outcomes, 63, 65–6, 70, 86
  poorly designed, 123
  process vs. aha, 36
  rules, 66–8
  types, 86
puzzle box, 25, 28–35
puzzle hunt, 25, 35–8, 114

QR codes, 28

real–world concepts, 65–6
red herrings (avoiding), 65, 69–70, 80, 91, 96, 123
red reveal, 27–8, 48
reflection, 4, 21, 35, 55, 103, 114, 127–8, 132–4, 152–3
rewards, 114–115
research challenge, 3, 8, 43, 87–8, 109–110
RFID tag, 74
role playing, 3, 49,75, 99–102
round–robin
  see stations

safety, 132
searching, 2, 47–9, 88, 109
self, 20–1
semaphore, 98
serial story, 25, 38–40
setting, 9–10, 47–9
sign language, 99
signposting, 72, 78, 89, 96
simulation, 19–20
skills, 15–16
Social Constructionism (theory), 2
social interactions, 11–12, 20–1
stations, 33–5
strategy, 17–8
story, 13–4, 38–40, 53–4, 56–8
story beats, 55–6
storyworld, 14, 46, 142–3

task, 15
team bonding, 11, 137
Thiagarajan, Sivasailam (Thiagi), 133
three-act structure, 54–5, 117–118
time limit, 4, 13, 54, 112–114, 126, 130, 132, 134
trivia
  see factual puzzles

UV light, 78

video, 59, 111–112, 127
virtual
  see digital tools
Vygotsky, Lev, 115–116

Wurman, Richard, 76
word puzzles, 86–8
worksheets (avoiding), 31,76, 95

Zone of Proximal Development, 115–116